TABLE OF CONTENTS

Introduction

Part I: Why Is Letting Go So Hard?

Chapter I: Guilt

Chapter II: Sunk Cost

Chapter III: Recoup The Cost

Chapter IV: Purposeless Practicality

Chapter V: Future Fear

Chapter VI: Sentimentality

Chapter VII: Perceived Value To Someone Else

Chapter VIII: Want to Dispose of Safely or Smartly

Part II: How to Tackle Five Tough Categories

Chapter I: Clothing

Chapter II: Books

Chapter III: Collections and Memorabilia

Chapter IV: Photographs

Chapter V: Paperwork

Conclusion

APPENDIX: Clever Girl's Cheat Sheet

Introduction

If you're reading this book, it's probably because you've been thinking about getting organized, decluttering or downsizing, and it hasn't been working out as you hoped. It's been harder to let go of things than you thought, or maybe it is *exactly* as hard as you thought it would be. Maybe you picked it up because you thought some secrets to success are in these pages. Perhaps you received this book as a gift from someone who loves you and sees you struggling. It may even be the tenth book on this topic you've tried to read, but, for some reason, this one looked like it might be different.

I believe it IS different. I believe you'll agree.

If you speak with a professional organizer about the struggles people have with letting things go, there's a good chance you'll hear the phrase, *"It's not about the stuff."* This book will explain what that means, as we get underneath the stuff, and understand and face the barriers that people build, in their heads and in their hearts, even when they merely LOOK at their stuff.

However, this is not a book that is going to tell you *"it's simple: just get rid of everything you don't use."* The goal is to help people who have already decided they WANT to live with less, want to have a less chaotic, less cluttered, less stressful life. Yet, though they know that letting go of some of their possessions will help them get there, they keep running into barriers that stop them. It is for people who know their possessions are standing in the way of living the life they desire, but they can't seem to break free from their stuff.

Breaking free requires doing things differently than we have before. We already know that doing more of the same only gets us, well, more of the same. In the case of letting things go, it means making a change in our *relationship* to stuff and thinking very differently about what we own and why we own it. My approach to this shift in thinking is based on moving from *"status quo possession"* to *"purposeful possession."*

Status quo possession says: *"There's nothing wrong with it, no good reason to let go of it, so I can just keep it, keep the status quo."* It becomes something that remains just because there isn't a compelling reason for it not to be there anymore. Purposeful possession, however, challenges your reasoning from *"why let it go?"* to *"why keep it at all?"* It calls for a reason, a purpose, for keeping it. Purposeful possession declares: *"I'm only going to keep the things that I truly love and use, the things that serve my current life and foreseeable future."*

That doesn't mean abandoning all you own, or that every possession must be reconsidered. If something isn't causing a problem for you, then maybe it's not something that needs to be tackled. You don't need to start making change by declaring war on all of your stuff. You can begin by evaluating your possessions and your spaces in the areas which you stand the most to gain. Find the problems that are causing you to want to make a change and live differently.

What might these problems look like?

- You've run out of storage or surface space and you're not getting more, at least, not without an investment of money or moving.
- You're struggling financially, but still spending money on things you don't need, or replacing items you've lost or have become damaged due to mishandling, creating deeper financial issues.
- You can't find the things you want because they're hidden behind or among the things you don't.
- You have the right things, but you have more than you need, and that overabundance is impacting your ability to hold onto other things.
- Your safety in your home is at risk, as you must navigate through things to get in, out, or through your home.
- You're embarrassed to have people over to your home, but you wish you could have people over to your home.
- Your relationships with others are suffering due to your attachment to things and how it impacts the quality of life in your home.
- You're distracted or overwhelmed by the clutter around you,

and it leaves you unmotivated or unable to get important things done in those spaces.

- You lament and resent that you're stressed out and spending and wasting too much time every day on keeping up and maintaining stuff.
- You're just not happy when you look around and see your home as it is today. You feel like there's no way out.

In my business, I work side by side with people who have identified their problems and declared, *"I want to make a change. I don't want my home and my life to feel like this anymore."* They believe their challenge is just that they don't know where to start or that they don't have organizing skills. It is only after we start looking more closely at the *"why"* that they begin to understand the *"how"* to moving forward and achieving their goals.

Decluttering or letting go of things is like any other change in your life: You must really want it, and you must know why you want it. **You have already begun to recognize that *"stuff"* is what is standing between you and the way you want to live your life.** You have made the declaration that you want to change, but still find so many reasons to hold onto the things that fill your home and your life. You must be able to face the question: *"What am I willing to change in order to live the way I want to?"* This book will help you get unstuck and get out of your own way to move forward and live that life.

This book is separated into two parts. In Part I, we're starting with *"why."* Why is letting go so hard? Even when you know you want to pare down, downsize, or live a less cluttered and chaotic life, your own thoughts can get in the way. You hold onto things because you have convinced yourself not to let go. You keep facing roadblocks and barriers, barriers that stop you in your tracks and prevent you from moving or even seeing past them. The result is that you're still surrounded by items that, deep down, you know you don't need, and could or would be happier if there was less of it around you.

We're going to explore the eight most common psychological and emotional barriers people experience, with some specific tools and tactics to keep in mind when you run into one of these barriers. You will see reminders in these chapters of purposeful possession and encouraging you to think differently about why you own things and using this framework as the beginning to each of the barriers.

In Part II, we shift to the "*how*" as we apply the new knowledge to tackling the five categories of "*stuff*" I find most people struggle with in their homes. We'll pinpoint the most common barriers that arise in each, and apply the practical techniques and approaches we've discussed, how to overcome them so that they are no longer too overwhelming to tackle.

By the time you're done with this book, you'll not only be armed with new strategies to lead this change, you may even *look forward* to decluttering the most complex spaces in your life and breaking free from your stuff!

PART I

WHY IS LETTING GO SO HARD?

Part I: Why Is Letting Go So Hard?

It can be frustrating to have all the intention in the world to take steps to declutter and reduce your stress, and then realize just how hard it is to let go of your things. Others around you may not appreciate what's going on inside you when you try to let go, and you may not even get it yourself. It feels like you're working against yourself, an internal argument, and you don't even really know why it is so hard. Understanding yourself, and what is going on in your head and in your heart, is the first step to moving past those challenges and accomplishing your goals.

To do that, we're going to discuss the psychological and emotional barriers that arise and stand in our way of letting go. They're not damning or deadly sins; they are merely the pulls and pushes that you feel that make the idea of letting go of items harder than they might be for someone else. The barriers appear as voices in our heads, ones we have imaginary arguments with as we're trying to make decisions. I tell my clients that these are "*the things that make your stuff sticky,*" as if they cause items to stick to your hands as you try to let them go. These are the factors that make it too difficult for you to put in a pile other than "*Keep.*"

The eight barriers I see most often:

1) **Guilt:** "*I'd feel too guilty to let go of this.*"

2) **Sunk Cost:** "*I paid good money for this.*"

3) **Recoup the Cost:** "*I could sell this*" or "*this is worth something.*"

4) **Purposeless practicality:** "*This is still good.*"

5) **Future Fear:** "*I might need it someday.*"

6) **Sentimentality:** "*It reminds me of a time,*" or "*It reminds me of someone,*" or "*I wouldn't want to forget...*"

7) **Perceived value to someone else:** "*I could give this as a gift,*" or "*I want this to go to someone who will appreciate it*" or "*My kids will want this.*"

8) **Want to Dispose of it Safely or Smartly:** "*I don't want it to go

in a landfill," or *"I don't know how to get rid of this safely, so I'll just hold onto it."*

You may see yourself in one of them; you may see a family member in another. You may not even realize some are issues for you if you haven't yet begun your dive into decluttering. They're the phrases that come up, either silently or out loud, that start with the word, **"but,"** as in *"but, I don't want to let go of this because… (insert reason here)."* Whatever comes up for you, you'll find help, answers, and maybe even more questions, to help you get to the bottom of your barrier, and move past it to success.

A way to get the most out of Part I is to have a peek into what Part II will bring. We'll be exploring strategies and practical techniques, the "how," that you can bring to five specific categories people tend to struggle with most often:

1) Clothes
2) Books
3) Collections and Memorabilia
4) Photos
5) Paperwork

When you reach Part II, you will already have read the psychological and emotional barriers that get in your way for these kinds of categories; these techniques will help you build a plan for success. They will help you come at this challenge from different directions, keep you on track, and focus on achieving your goals.

Throughout Part I, I hope you find yourself, your thoughts, your words, in some of these barriers, and can start applying the strategies and tools to help dismantle them. As you address barrier after barrier, you should feel inspired and armed to take action, meaningful action, as you begin to reduce the items around you, and live with less.

Chapter I: Guilt

"I can't. I'd feel guilty if I let this go."

We're starting with guilt? Already? Yes. We're starting with guilt because it's one of the most common barriers for people. I hear it in so many forms, including:

"But it was a gift."

"But my child made this for me."

"But this meant a lot to my aunt. She's passed away now. I feel like I'd be betraying her memory."

"But he took the time to do this for me."

These "*but*" statements are guilt coming to the surface. We know how it feels and we know how strong it can be when it shows up.

Why is the barrier, **Guilt**, so strong? It attaches like gravity to the item, and makes it so much harder to let go of, doesn't it?

First, let's talk about what the emotion of guilt is. It is an internal barometer we have, that helps us see when our actions are not matching up to our values, and psychological discomfort is created. In general, this is a helpful tool; it is part of how we self-regulate as we make choices between right and wrong. This emotion helps us understand when our actions may have an impact on others that we otherwise would not intend. In short, guilt can be a good thing.

Of course, it can also get in our way, especially when that concern about harming others is not in line with reality. Sometimes it is a question of *"will this even hurt someone else?"* and sometimes, further, *"yes, but how deeply will it hurt them?"* We can feel guilt for things other than people, such as feeling like our actions harm the planet or environment (Chapter VIII is about this).

If guilt is causing us to hold onto things that we no longer value, we may really be saying, *"I'm afraid of hurting the feelings of someone else or doing damage to someone or something I care about, <u>even if they never know</u> I took this action."* We fear that someone else will feel rejected, betrayed, disregarded, harmed if we let go of a thing.

Not hurting others sounds like an admirable goal, though, doesn't it? If the emotion of guilt is preventing someone from hurting others, why is this a problem?

There are two ways in which this creates a problem and gets in our way. The first arises when the protection of feelings of others, real or imagined feelings, becomes more important than self-preservation or our own goals of how we want to live. When guilt dominates our actions, especially guilt based on an unrealistic fear of consequence, it can make it challenging, if not impossible, to pursue competing and valuable goals. *"I want to declutter and live a less chaotic life. But I can't do that because I am holding onto these things that aren't at all important to me, because I want to avoid the negative feelings that come up when I imagine letting it go."* See that barrier go right up?

The second problem is created when the fear of consequence is often unrealistic or not aligned with the action. We've exaggerated in our minds the potential outcome of our action (*"They'll hate me!" "They'll judge me!" "They'll never let me live this down!" "They'll think I don't appreciate them!"*) and this exaggerated impact becomes the terrorizing voice in our head. So, instead we have a shortcut in our brains that tells us, *"I care about this person, and that person cares about me, so, I couldn't possibly let go of this greeting card she sent me six years ago, because that would send a message that I didn't care."* This disconnect between imagined outcome and likely reality can cause the Guilt barrier to take over.

Guilt shows up reviewing items you own in so many categories, but I want to focus on just a few:

- items you've received for free from others,
- heirlooms or possessions you've inherited, and
- gifts, the biggest category.

Guilt about items you've received for free from others. These aren't standard gifts, with thought and meaning behind them. These are the *"Hey, I was cleaning out my garage and had this thing I was getting rid of. I thought* *you might be able to use it*" or "*My son has outgrown his toys, and I thought your son might appreciate them.*" Someone else's hand-me-downs or cast-offs come your way, well-intentioned, and the burden is placed on you to either reject it or accept it graciously.

There are a few reasons why this is tricky. The first is an obvious one: Who doesn't like free stuff? Acquiring something that may be useful, and for free no less, sounds like a win at the time. In fact, this "*win*" can override any other measurement of how much we might value the item. We may think, "*I'd never pay for this, because it isn't worth my money to acquire it. But if it is free, it could be valuable to me.*" There is something to be said, however, for the critical thinking that goes along with acquiring an item when we have to pay for it. When we must pay money for something, we can evaluate whether we'll use it, take care of it, etc. If something comes along as free, we can ignore the other costs that go along with it, when money isn't one of them. We might not think of whether we will use it, or have space to store it, or the ability to maintain it properly. We're blinded by the price tag.

When the true cost appears, the burden they can create in our lives can be met with guilt in the concept of letting it go after saying yes. It can be caused by accepting just one item or by the pile than can grow from continuously accepting these items. It travels back to our feeling for the person who gave us the item, and the social contract we created when we accepted the item. We can feel like we're letting the other person down or betraying them when, in the end, we choose to no longer keep the item, either because we can't or we just don't want to.

The other part of the guilt that goes along with this exchange is that we can recognize that the givers may have made difficult decisions to let the items go, or are going on a decluttering journey, and we like them and want to support them. We say yes because we'd feel guilty to say no. We can take on an obligation to honor someone else's thoughtful act, and someone else's desire to achieve his or her own decluttering goals. "*If I take this from her, she'll feel better about letting it go. If I can help her by doing that, then I will.*"

I hope you can see that, again, the guilt is related to feelings about the person, and the item becomes representative of the positive feelings you have about the person. You pay the price, one box or shelf at a time, what you're willing to sacrifice space in your home to preserve and honor that relationship.

Guilt from heirlooms or inherited possessions. This category covers both items that have been passed down and specifically set aside for you, or the situation that comes when someone passes or moves and leaves behind many things, not necessarily valuable possessions, but their remaining belongings. Each has its own trickiness to deal with when it comes to guilt.

Heirlooms passed down through generations, tend to be items that we have attached some value to, either financial or sentimental. They are unique or represent moments in a family's history that feel iconic, marked with a physical, material object. Jewelry, serving items (china, crystal, silver, etc.), military medals, books, furniture, family bibles, artwork, tools, the list goes on and on. We attach importance to these items, often because importance was attached to them before we owned them. These items become something we not only possess but honor. Parents, grandparents, and great-grandparents saved possessions at a time when *how* and *why* we acquired things were very different. Things were either necessities or luxuries. Luxuries often represented sacrifice and special occasions, and therefore, they were viewed with greater importance.

As time has gone on, our own ability to acquire things has changed, and the percentage of items we'd consider a necessity or a luxury worth sacrifice has become a smaller percentage of what we acquire. We bring in more convenience, impulse, and immediate-satisfaction items, more inexpensive-and-replaceable items. In some ways, this perspective actually makes those heirlooms feel even more special, inflating the rareness and value of the item as we compare it to how things come into our lives today.

All that said, it can be hard to look at a thing and evaluate it for what it truly is, removing the heirloom title from it, stripping the honor we've bestowed upon an inanimate object. This part of the barrier arrives for us when we look at that possession objectively and say, *"The only reason I am holding onto this is that it was important to someone else in the past. Maybe even important to me, because it was important to them. But now, it is just a thing that doesn't serve me, may even take valuable space away from me, or cost me to insure or maintain it. I no longer love or want it, but... well, it's an heirloom."* How it came to be ours becomes the sole weight of the item.

The other items that come into our lives in a similar way are the remaining belongings of a loved one. These can be a challenge because they seem to represent who the people were on this earth, a collection of their daily lives, their hobbies, their accomplishments. It is often of great comfort to hold onto items after someone passes away, but over time, as we mourn and grieve, the need for that comfort, and the comfort these items bring can fade. When the emotions are no longer as strong, it is easier to objectively review what is there to be discovered. When I work with clients on this process, we'll find useful things, valuable things, and things no one in a million years would deem as *"special"* but in cleaning out a drawer or a cabinet or a closet, it wound up in the full collection. (Did you really need to pack Uncle Joe's old undershirts?)

There is absolutely no doubt that people need time before addressing these items. When struggling with a loss, there are so many other emotions to face. It may take a great deal of time before taking steps that require separating feelings for the person from feelings for the possessions.

In some of these cases, we look through someone else's belongings and just don't know what's important, meaningful, or valuable. We may never have been told or been given directions on how to evaluate all that comes our way. (This is good to keep in mind as you think about what you leave behind for your loved ones. Help others understand what you're leaving behind and what it means, so that they may better appreciate the items and honor them the way you'd hope.)

With either the heirlooms or the larger set of every-day possessions, what we have ended up taking responsibility for is the evidence of other people's passions and priorities. *"Uncle Joe collected old radios. So, I guess now, I too, have a collection of old radios, because I have his. They were important to him, and he was important to me, so this is something I now need to maintain."* These were their memories, passions, and priorities. They are not *your* memories, passions, and priorities.

With these heirlooms and possessions, it can be hard to say, *"I'm choosing my own passions over what yours were. I'm choosing my own styles over what yours were. I'm choosing the items that I love over the items that you loved,"* without feeling selfish, feeling guilty. It feels like we are dishonoring people who mattered to us, when we don't hold onto the things that may (or may not) have mattered to them. The guilt barrier kicks in when something in our hearts says to us, *"If you really loved this person, you'd keep this stuff, no matter what negative impact it has on your life."* And at that moment, as you hear your own voice, **"...no matter what negative impact it has on your life..."** you should ask yourself, *"Would that person want me to resent his stuff? Would that person want me to feel burdened to own this and maintain it?"* You already know the answer is "Of course not." At that moment, you can see that your honor and love can be mutual, even after they've passed. You can let go of the things that feel burdensome to you, because they would not want to be the source of burden on you, ever.

Gift guilt. This is perhaps the strongest builder of that guilt barrier. Whenever you are decluttering and come across a gift you've received, or even if you're just dealing with the immediate reaction of opening a gift that just isn't a forever-keeper for you, guilt becomes a major factor.

First, I want you to think about the process you go through when selecting and giving a gift. In many cases, you put a lot of thought and effort into finding and giving the gift, because you wanted the receiver to feel loved and valued. It was a gesture of your feelings for them. Or, maybe you actually DIDN'T put in that much effort; you had some generic gifts ready to give, or you went and got something that could work for just about anyone, because you wanted, or felt like you had to, provide a gesture. **Either way, when you went through the process, you probably weren't thinking**:

> *"I hope this makes this person feel guilty, and that she or he ends up struggling with whether to keep it, now or in the future. I hope this gift ends up being a burden on them. I hope they feel bad every time they see it. I hope they keep shoving it in a drawer or a cabinet, or put it on a shelf to dust for years, purely because they'd rather not upset me."*

Of course, you weren't. Neither were the people who gave you gifts. Yet you are creating this imaginary conversation in your head with them that assumes they were? (Okay, I'll acknowledge that there are people who give some *"loaded"* gifts, where the giver has ulterior motives, and if you feel guilty that might be okay with them, but we're not here to talk about them; that one is for your therapist!)

I want to help you understand and untangle the guilt, reframe the conversation in your head, let go of the gift that is holding you back, and prepare for the conversation you might be dreading with the gift giver.

What causes the guilt in the exchange of gifts? What are those voices in our head saying that makes it hard for us to let go of the item? Sometimes, it's about *the gift*, and sometimes, it is about *the giver*:

The Gift:

- It's not your style, but the person who gave it to you thought you'd like it.
- It used to be your style, but isn't anymore, and the person who gave it thought it still was.
- It makes you feel judged or bad about yourself, like the membership to the gym you didn't ask for or want.
- It's great, but you just don't have the room.
- It's great, but there are limitations in your life that prevent you from using it. For instance, it requires moving or lifting, or reaching, but you're not able to physically manage it.
- You love it, but it will require you to spend money to upkeep and maintain it. And maybe you don't have that money, or, if you do, you wouldn't spend it on this. I call this the *"Surprise! I bought you a puppy!"* scenario.
- It was a wedding gift. You registered for it. Someone got it because you said you wanted it. You've changed your mind since then.
- The gift clearly means more to the gift giver for you to have it than it does to you.
- It was obviously expensive, and the gift giver doesn't have a lot of money, and you know this set that person back a bit to give it.
- It was expensive, and it has value. You feel like you're making a bad choice when letting go of something that was expensive.

- It was great, and you loved it for a long time, but you've outgrown it.
- And, probably another dozen answers….

The Giver:

- You love and respect the giver, and don't want to hurt his or her feelings by rejecting or letting go of a gift that came from a kind gesture.
- It was a surprise to receive a gift from the giver; Receiving it was lovely and humbling. The gesture, but not the gift, was meaningful.
- You're not actually a huge fan of the gift giver, and looking at the gift reminds you of that, and brings up negativity.
- The giver has since passed away, and it feels disrespectful to let something go that he or she gave you. Holding onto it means honoring the memory of that person. You feel better and closer to that person because you have a thing that she or he gave you, even if the item itself isn't important.
- You'd rather keep the thing than have a difficult conversation with that gift giver about why you don't have it anymore. You've decided you'll display it only when they come over, just in case they look for it. You'll sacrifice the space it takes to hold onto the thing and just live with disappointment and avoid confrontation or making them feel bad.

Gifts, as you can see, can be so tangled with emotion about the items and the people behind them. No wonder the guilt barrier is so strong!

For all three categories – hand-me-downs, heirlooms, and gifts – the guilt voice can be powerful, and requires a strong internal (and sometimes external) counter argument to help you retain focus on your own goals, your own priorities, and be able to push past the guilt barrier. **You know the imaginary conversation in your head is strong, and you need to stand up to that voice in your head.** Here are some responses that can work for your internal argument:

- "*I can be grateful for the thought, which, after all, is what counts. I can be grateful for the gift giver. That doesn't mean I must ALSO be grateful for, and obligated to permanently own, the gift itself.*"

- "*The gift giver never intended to give me a gift that feels like a burden, or causes a problem for me and my home. They did it because they wanted to share a gesture of something positive, and would hate knowing that it did the opposite.*"

- "*I, and not the gift giver or the hand-me-down giver or the heirloom passer, gets to decide what I keep in my home, where I keep it, and for how long.*"

- "*Not all gifts land perfectly. I'm sure I've given some things that just were not so great, either. I wouldn't want someone holding onto a gift they didn't love, just because they thought it would upset me if they didn't.*"

- "*The value of items I've received can expire, can have a shelf life. I enjoyed it at the time. I really did. I'm thankful to the person who brought this to my life for that. But I just don't get out of it what I did then, and it's okay to move it along.*" This is easier to see with items like a baby toy, but your child is now 6, or a clothing item that just doesn't fit you anymore, or a hobby that you just aren't into anymore.

- "*Someone else will love this item way more than I do. Why am I holding onto it, without getting anything positive in my life from it, when someone else would be thrilled to have it?*"

- "*Honestly, I could return this or sell this and get something I truly DO love, which I expect is what the person who brought this to my life really wanted to feel.*"

- "*This is an heirloom piece, and I know that someone else in my family would love the opportunity to have this for a while.*"

Great! You've won your imaginary argument, and you are convinced! You've moved the item to the donate box, or to the "*give to someone else I know*" box, or the "*I'm returning or selling this*" pile or maybe even the circular "*no one is going to want this*" receptacle near the door.

But you're still wary of the real-life conversation with the person to whom you feel guilty. The conversation may be a proactive one, as when you need to ask for a gift receipt or you want to give the gift giver right of first refusal on taking it back. It may be a reactive one, like declining the offer of some hand-me-downs, or addressing it when someone asks, "*Whatever happened to that chafing dish I gave you?*" Either way, finding the right and most respectful words is important. You'll find your own words, I'm sure, but maybe these will help:

- "*Mom, I've had Aunt Jane's tea set for many years, but I just don't use it like she probably hoped I would. I think someone else in the family would enjoy having it more than I do right now. Do you have any thoughts on who would love honoring this heirloom next?*"

- "*I loved having this in my home when I had more space, but now I have to make some difficult decisions about what stays here. It's time for me to let it go to someone who will love it as much as I did when I first received it. I wanted to make sure, though, that if you wanted it for yourself, that I offered it to you. Would you like it?*"

- "*What a thoughtful gift this is! It means a lot to me that you thought of me during the holidays. Unfortunately, it's just not what I'm wearing/ using/ listening to these days. Would you be okay if I exchanged it for something I had my heart set on?*"

- "*I love that you remembered how much I have always enjoyed _____. I have fond memories of it, too, but it's just not as big a part of my life as it once was. You're so thoughtful to have given me this, and I've decided to pass it along, just as thoughtfully, to someone else who will be thrilled to have it.*"

- *"You are always so considerate of me when you're going through your own things. I have absolutely appreciated your generosity! Right now, however, I just don't need this item you're giving me, and I'm trying to do much better at saying no to things in my life that I don't need and take space, which is kind of at a premium for me. I am sure you'll find someone else who can use this item more than I can!"*

- *"Where is the _____ you got us? I recently went through so many things, to get my life more calm and enjoyable, and remove the things that were causing me stress. I found that I had a lot of items I was holding onto that I didn't love or use anymore, and I was holding onto them just because I loved the person who gave it to me. I finally came to my senses and realized that I wouldn't want someone I loved to hold onto things, just because they loved me back. So, a lot of things went, and that ____ was one of them. I enjoyed having it for the time I did, and I'm glad to know someone else is probably enjoying it even more right now."*

That wasn't so painful now, was it? It may have stung a little, but remember, this is about <u>preserving the way you want to live in your home</u>, and what you want to be surrounded with when you're there.

And, while you're at it, model good guiltless behavior towards others:

- Be a better gift giver. Give experiences, give gifts that you know are needed and wanted, give gifts that aren't going to become clutter.

- Whenever possible, include gift receipts, and maybe a little note that says *"If this gift doesn't surprise and delight you, make sure you get yourself something that does."*

- Teach your kids how to be grateful, gracious, but not to associate the value of the gift with the value of the giver. Guilt is an emotion that we start to learn at an early age. If you find yourself saying, *"Oh, but you can't get rid of that; your great-aunt gave it to you,"* check with yourself if that is the guilt talking, and if that is what you want to teach your kids to associate with letting go.

- When you're going through your own things and creating a *"give to someone else pi*le," do everything you can to ensure your gesture of generosity doesn't come with a sense of burden, guilt, or convincing appeal. Don't give the kind of gift that would make someone say yes to an item, purely because they want to say yes to YOU, not the thing.

- Don't ask others what they did with YOUR gift... *"hey... where is that Bass-o-Matic I got you for your wedding?"*

Chapter II: Sunk Cost

"I paid good money for this."

"This cost a lot."

You look at an item, one you know you aren't using these days, or don't love, or have some other response that makes you think, *"I don't need this and should let this go."* Along comes the barrier: You remember how expensive it was, or how much you paid for it, and you stop in your tracks. You are wary of letting go of an item because you are reminded of how much it cost to obtain it in the first place.

This is called a **sunk-cost attachment**, where you are focused more on how much you paid for something in the past than on what you will get out of it in the future. When your brain throws up this barrier, it takes you right back to the decision-making process you went through the day you acquired it, regardless of the value it currently holds in your life or for your future. That barrier is taking you back in time to challenge your thought process from the day the item came into your life.

Whether you purchased it, asked someone else for it, accepted it from someone, or found it on the street, however it came into your life, you're remembering what went into the process owning it. You're recalling the pros and cons list that came up when you decided to get it. You may have waffled, or you may have been very clear, but there was a reason behind making this choice. Maybe it was:

- Something you viewed as an investment for the future.

- Something you viewed as fully worth it at the time, but you are now seeing that it has served its purpose, it doesn't serve you anymore, or you're ready for something new to replace it.

- A splurge, a treat for yourself, because at the time you felt you deserved it.

- An impulse-buy that caught your eye.

- A fad that you swore wouldn't be a fad.

- A fad that you knew would be a fad but had to have it anyway.
- Something that was a risk: *"This might work for us; I'll buy it and return it if it doesn't."* You didn't.
- Something for which you had to sacrifice or make difficult choices to get it, and you feel an obligation to the item because of what you sacrificed.
- A purchase someone else tried to tell you that it might not be a good idea, and you hear, *"I told you so,"* when you look at it.
- An item you imagined at the time would be valued tremendously (*"I'll wear this suit all the time!"*) but that vision didn't pan out.

When reactions like these come up, you're fixating on the thought process that went on in your head when you decided to move forward with it. Now, as you face the choice to let go of it, your brain is trying to remind you of all the reasons you once thought this was a good idea, and convince you it is still a good idea today: *"You decided already to get this. You traded money that you could have done something else with but didn't. That's a good enough reason to keep this. Forever and ever and ever."*

Your brain is fixated on the COST, not the VALUE. It is focusing on the outlay of money or space or sacrifice that went into that exchange. Value, however, is what you *get* for the choice you made, and it doesn't always work out in our favor. When we're honest with ourselves, we can identify that there is a big difference between cost and value and that there are many things in our life that show us how big that difference can be.

Let's walk through an example of how this comes to life. You have two shirts in your closet hanging next to each other. One shirt you purchased for $10, and the other you spent $75 on, a splurge from your typical spending habits. You wear the $10 shirt all the time, maybe even weekly. The $75 shirt? You wore it once, or maybe never and it still has the tags attached.

Consider this:
The $10 shirt is more valuable to you than the $75 shirt.

If you wear your $10 shirt all the time, it has more value in your life (value for clothes = wear-ability) than the $75 shirt you thought you'd wear but never did. But you convinced yourself the day you bought it that you would wear it, that you would love it, that you would get a lot of use out of it.

In fact, that $75 shirt has a NEGATIVE value in your life, because not only is the shirt not contributing to your life as a wearable shirt, it's also taking up space from one that could be worn, or just space that doesn't have to be filled at all. Or it's getting in your way, physically and mentally, when you look through your closet to find something to wear, and it just hangs there, maybe in your way, like a flag waving and saying, "*Not me! Not going to wear me, yet again...*" (If the tags are still on it, it's shouting it even louder.) It is as if it is flaunting how little value it has in your current life, regardless of the cost of acquiring it in the first place.

Not to say this is only about making decisions that didn't pan out. Definitely not! The "*I paid good money for this*" barrier can come up when something that HAS been valuable, used, and loved. Sometimes, that $75 shirt was worn a lot, so much that it, well, looks well-worn, and not in a good way. It's no longer in good shape, and it's obvious. Perhaps it doesn't fit anymore, and isn't likely to ever again. Or, it is significantly out of style, and not likely to come back in style anytime soon, or in your lifetime. Still, you're reminded of the cost it took to acquire, and not the value it plays in your current life or foreseeable future, and in your closet, it stays.

Tackling this barrier comes first and foremost from recognizing it when it occurs. When you're aware that you're talking about cost and not value, you can start to untangle the conversation. Why?

First, you'll be able to remind yourself that the money is gone, and it doesn't come back to you just because you continue to hold onto the thing. While, yes, a few items can appreciate in value over time, most of what you would consider clutter as you look around your home probably doesn't fall into that category. Accepting the reality that the money is gone is the first step.

Second, it allows you to step back and determine the *current value*. How is this item serving you today? What positive role is it playing in your current life?

Third, with the value side of the equation established, you can identify objectively the ways it negatively contributes to your life today. These are the *current costs*, not the initial financial investment you made in acquiring it. It takes up space, space that may be more valuable to you if used in a different way. It requires maintenance. It is something you need to move out of the way to get to the things you want or need. It reminds you of the weight you've gained and then you get depressed. It prevents you from putting something else you love in that space. What are *your* negatives? What does owning this item cost you today, besides the money you paid for it in the first place?

When you go through these steps, you are wrestling the conversation away from the "*buy me*" moment in the past, and bringing it to today's terms. You are shifting the balance equation now to: "*Does the* **current** *value outweigh the* **current** *costs to my life?*" You remove the influence of the initial investment in your decision-making, remove the influence of the past and what you once imagined the future would hold.

I loved a story I once heard that helps illustrate this point: "*If I pay for a movie ticket, and 20 minutes into the movie I can tell that it's horrible and not worth my time, why would I spend the next 2 hours sitting there? It has already taken my money... why would I also give it my time and energy to continue to commit to the choice?*" The cost of the ticket is a sunk cost, and there is probably nothing else you can do about that. Anything else you give to it from that point on is on you.

Tearing down this barrier requires valuing your current quality of life more than you value the decisions of the past. It is tough work, but the fresh perspective can help you unlock the success of achieving your goal of living with less.

Chapter III: Recoup The Cost

> *"This is valuable. A collector's item.
> Somebody will want this."*
>
> *"I could get some money for this."*
>
> *"I don't want to just give it away for free
> if I can get something for it."*

This one is related to the sunk cost barrier, *"I paid good money for this,"* but while that one is about your brain putting up a fight around letting go, this one is further down the path. With the **recoup the cost** barrier, you're open to the idea of letting it go, but now you're focusing on how sweet the circumstances must be to do so. You're imagining what you could receive as compensation in exchange for it. There is a negotiator in your head making the decisions around *how* you let go of it. Your brain is saying, *"I'll let this go, if you can convince me I will be rewarded, or at least that I won't be negatively impacted financially if I do so. I don't want to miss out on something I'm owed."*

You start to hear the bargaining thoughts come up in your head. If we were in a cartoon, you'd blink and have dollar signs on your eyeballs. You mentally place a price tag, either with a specific dollar amount or a mystery price, on the item, and you start to cling to it a bit more. You may not have even thought of it in a long time, but now that you hold it and you think *"I can exchange this for money,"* your inner negotiator, and occasionally a stubborn one, takes over.

There is certainly a chance that things you own may be exchangeable for money somewhere. However, your desire to recoup the cost becomes a barrier when:

> 1) With no sales or real plan to sell in place, the lack of action to sell the items leads to a growing pile that restricts how you want to use the space around you.
>
> 2) You continue to hold onto items, despite evidence that they are not selling through conventional or even targeted sales approaches, with no alternative exit strategy. An exit strategy is a plan you have

that brings an end or exit to those times out of your life.

3) The value of the space, time, and energy you're allotting to the possessions exceeds the value you could receive by selling them.

You must determine if your desire to sell an item is realistic. If it isn't, it is critical to recognize you are creating your own barrier by holding onto the idea of selling, and you must set that dream aside if you wish to move past the barrier.

When that moment comes where you think, "*I can sell this*," respond back to your inner negotiator with a few questions:

- Is that *really* true? How do you know? Do you have a good sense of the current market and value for that item? Do you know the demand for it? Is it in the kind of shape and condition the market values and will pay for?

- Is going through the process of trying to sell it worth your time? Getting it ready may mean research, pictures, descriptions, trying to arrange with people for deals that fall through, fighting off scam inquiries, and your time and energy. Is what you think you're going to get from this item worth all that to you?

- Is focusing on the idea that you can sell things getting in your way of progress towards your goal of decluttering or reducing the chaos in your life?

- Do you know how to sell? If you think "*oh, this can sell on eBay or Craigslist or online somewhere,*" but you don't actually know how to do that technologically speaking, what is your plan on how to make it happen? Are you willing to pay someone else to do it for you? Is the net cost, after you pay that person, going to be worth it?

- Can you make this process time-bound and set deadlines? "*If I don't sell it in the next two weeks, I'll donate it,*" or "*If I list it online and it doesn't sell after 2 weeks, I'll assume no one will be asking for it and I'll let it go*" are ways of setting boundaries and moving to action.

- Are you better off or at least close enough to your expectations of how much you could get for it to instead donate the item and take a tax deduction?

- Is there more value in just passing this item along to help others? Can being generous to others be a motivating factor to remind you that you can let something go, even if you don't get money for it? If you've benefited from the generosity of others in the past, is this an opportunity to pay it forward?

When you work through the set of practical questions, it can help you put your aspirations about sales into perspective. You may be able to have a feasible plan of action, and make progress towards your goal of living with less. Alternatively, these questions can help you get clear about why it may not be the right choice for how to deal with this item. You may learn, *"Yes, I could sell this item, but it's not worth it for me to do so, so I'm giving it away instead."* The barrier does not have to stand in your way anymore.

Tearing down this barrier can also bring some difficult emotions; in some ways, this barrier is protecting you from that. There may be feelings of loss, disappointment, maybe even rejection because people aren't valuing things you love in the same way you do. Avoiding these emotions may cause you to not face this issue. Keeping in mind your goals and why you're looking to live with less will continue to give you the reinforcement to face the tougher emotions that come your way when tearing down the barriers.

Chapter IV: Purposeless Practicality

"This is still good."

"This still works."

"This is broken, but could be fixed."

"This still has a little life in it."

This chapter is a little complex, because the barrier isn't *really* what we see on the surface. In this chapter, the barrier arrives once you look at something and say *"but, this is still good,"* and your analysis about it stops. The statement stops analyzing if it is something you need, or even want. As you hold the item, it seems hard for you to look past the idea that something which works or is in good shape must, by definition, be worth keeping.

Purposeless practicality is the barrier in which something *"perfectly good"* is practical, but serves no purpose for your current and foreseeable life. The antidote to the purposeless practicality barrier is embracing *purposeful possession*. It means being okay with saying, *"even if it's still good, if it isn't serving me, I can let it go."*

Obviously, there are items that mean more to you than their practical purpose when you look at them and answer those questions. This chapter isn't about those items (but the Sentimentality chapter is). This isn't about a hard and fast rule getting rid of everything you haven't touched in six months or more, either. This is about the items for which the only emotional attachment, if any, is about reflecting on your former pastimes or the dreams you once had for your future, and are taking up valuable space in your home, and in how you live *today* or your likely future.

The barrier, *"but this is still good,"* can stop you from being honest with yourself. This chapter is about the things you find and realize there's more to the eye than just the item. There's a story behind the item, often a story you've even forgotten was there.

Here's the kind of conversation in which this might come up when I am working with a client:

"I found your tennis rackets. Do you play tennis?"

"No. I used to. But this is a new one. Barely used it."

"Do you plan to play again?"

"No, but this is in good shape, so I should keep it."

When these items appear, there is a deeper level underneath that I often find when trying to help reveal why an item that isn't being used still can be so difficult to let go of. It's when the question gets asked, *"So, regardless of whether it is still good, why aren't you using it now? How did it come into your life, but isn't an active part of it now?"* This requires the ability to look past the item and its usefulness and really analyze and face how it came into a home, why it came into a home. More often, it is to those questions that we find the the real sticking point of the useful-but-not-used items.

Answering these questions often reveal a story that tells of the vision of that item and how it would be used, or how it once was used. These stories start with *"I used to use that"* or *"I used to be really into this"*, or they start with, *"I thought I'd be"* or *"I wanted to use it"*. Statements like these hearken up identities: past identities or future, imagined identities that never came to life.

That client stopped playing tennis for a reason. Thought she'd get back to it someday. Deep down, still does. She may be thinking that raising kids took her down a different path than she'd planned. All of these feelings might be lurking underneath that perfectly-good and unused tennis racket.

The *"I used to"* stories involve hobbies we once had, interests that we've moved on from, even jobs and relationships that are no longer part of our current lives. The items we're finding from those stories, which are still *"perfectly good"* are no longer being used because our life no longer requires them to be in it. They can be items, like CDs or books or movies or even clothing, that were a big part of your life and your interests at one point in time, but don't have any place in your current life, other than they've been allotted space in your home. They are the items we acquired along the way of living our lives, and have stayed around, even though our lives have long since changed beyond when they figured prominently. But, yes, *"they're still perfectly good."* That just isn't the question that needs to be asked. The questions now are:

    1) What role do these items *truly* play in your current life?

2) If the answer is "*none*" or "*minimal,*" why are you allowing it to take up valuable space in your home? Why are you making space in your real estate for something you no longer make space for in the way you live your life?

The "*I want to*" or "*I wanted to*" statements are attached to items that we *imagined* could be or would be part of our lives someday. The obvious examples are the treadmill we thought for sure we'd use because we were going to get in shape. The specialty cooking tools that we were *definitely* going to use more often. The dressy clothes we knew we were going to wear to a special occasion, but the tags are still on it. The tools in the garage we were going to use for a special project someday. Sometimes, heartbreak is attached, as with the nursery for the baby that never came to be. The future imagined visions of ourselves that have yet to happen, and may never. In fact, we may have long since moved past that vision for ourselves, but the stuff we acquired has stayed on the shelf, well, because "*they're still good.*"

When facing an item that's rooted in these distant past or imagined future, we're no longer evaluating the item; we're evaluating that vision for our lives. Instead of asking, "*is this tennis racket still good?*" let's ask, "*is playing tennis still a priority in my life? Do I have the time, the ability, the interest to continue to have that activity be a part of my life, one that requires me to hold onto all this equipment that goes with it? Is it still as important enough to me to store all this?*" Both halves of the question are critical:

1) Is it still a priority and does it genuinely fits into my life?

2) Is the only way for me to pursue this activity is by OWNING and STORING all these items that go with it?

Let's face it: If you say, "*yes, I still want to and can play tennis,*" you might also move that forward more practically with, "*but maybe only once a year, maybe even less often. I can rent or borrow a tennis racket the next time I play. In fact, I can rent a better one than I own now.*"

The same holds true for the items from your past as they do for the items for your once-imagined future. We know that the more the time has passed since you imagined this item being truly used in your life, the less likely it is you will get back to a point where it will be used. But the hard work is in looking at your current life and the *likely* future you'll have and determining whether this item and the vision you had for it still holds true. Is that vision still important to you? Is it still feasible? Do you still have the interest, the time, the energy, the money, whatever support you need to make it happen? The guitar you wanted for Christmas because you really wanted to learn guitar? It's been sitting there. Maybe even for years. Now it stares back at you, and you are brave enough to answer the question honestly: *Will I really study and learn how to play guitar?*

Facing this barrier can be particularly challenging because it can bring up a lot of emotion, and sometimes those emotions are ones we'd prefer to avoid at all costs. Understanding that those emotions exist, however, help get in touch with the *"why,"* and help you deal more rationally and move past these emotions:

- There can be guilt, related to your own underutilization of a practical item: *"I asked for this for a gift, and even though I lost interest, I feel bad because someone spent money on it."*

- There may be a feeling of failure, especially if that item relates to a vision you once had for your future: *"I feel like I'm giving up on a dream. Knowing I never pursued it, and likely never will, makes me sad, maybe even angry."*

- You may be mourning a loss of what your life used to be like. Maybe you were healthier, or had more money, or were more active. Maybe you had a career you enjoyed, but that's no longer your situation. Maybe you enjoyed activities with friends and family or romantic relationships, but that's not as much a part of your life anymore. Your life has changed, and these items are remnants that can cause you to say, *"This a sad or painful reminder how my life used to be and of what I've lost."*

- There may be a feeling of waste and regret. You spent money on things as an investment, maybe a gamble for what you thought you might do in the future. You were confident that it would be an expense you'd justify through action. However, you never took that action, or didn't take it as much as you thought you would when you made the purchase. If you happen to be struggling financially now, you may regret that you don't have that money now, and are left only with the item that you don't use. The reality and the feelings can be hard to face.

- There can be a sense of shame when you find an item, or multiples of them, were items you kept buying to replace the ones you couldn't find because your home was too disorganized.

- There can be shame or disappointment because you truly wanted or needed to change, and just didn't follow through. This is very common when coming across items that were meant to change bad habits: *"I bought this smoking cessation gum because I was going to quit, but now it is expired, and I never even tried it"* or *"I bought these workout clothes because I was going to get healthy, but I never did"* or *"I bought this book about getting organized but I never did anything with it and I'm still overwhelmed."* It can also come from the things that were meant to bring about a new lifestyle: *"I wore this suit at the interview for the job I didn't get"* or *"this suitcase was going to be for the traveling I wanted to do, but have never done."* You find these items to be reminders of all the things you said you'd achieve but never did.

- You may feel real sadness for the vision that never came to be, what you'd hoped your life would be like. You bought or held onto something because you hoped life would take you down a different path, one where you'd need it. But it didn't, and the item remained.

- There may be other emotions that this generates. Negative ones that make the process of going through this, quite frankly, we're all interested in avoiding if we can. But that's not being honest, and that's not making progress.

These emotions can be overwhelming when they come up. They can cause you to want to retreat from the tough work you're doing, going through your things to evaluate whether they have value now. When these emotions arise, remember: These are tough questions, and tough decisions to come to *about your life*, but you're going through this because you've already declared, *"I need to own less. I want to own less."* If you're committed to paring down and reducing what you own, but you're stuck letting go of items that are *"still good"*, it's important to get underneath not the practicality of the item and its potential usefulness, but truly the purpose it plays in your current life and your foreseeable future.

Chapter V: Future Fear

"I might need it someday."

These words have probably crossed your mind, and maybe your lips, when you've been going through the piles, the stacks, the shelves, the cupboards, the closets. Amazingly, these words have the power to paralyze forward movement and to make you fear an imagined life where *"needing it"* occurred, and you were left without it.

You may think, *"I might need this someday,"* and holding onto the item is just about being smart and being practical, and you're feeling good about holding onto things. It's actually not. The **future fear** barrier is really about *worry*, and it prevents you from making a choice based on logic or reason. You worry about a future you cannot predict and cannot control. You worry about being vulnerable or having a need you can't instantly meet. You feel that holding onto an item somehow helps you meet that imaginary need in your imaginary future, and you'll feel prepared, smart, resourceful, valuable, and just plain *"better"* than you would without it.

You worry that a time will come where you DO need something you once had, but you let go of it. If that happens, you will feel like past-you let future-you down by letting go of that item. You worry that you will regret your choice you make today, so you prefer to hold onto it, *"just to be sure,"* rather than value the goals you have for your space and your life today.

The barrier isn't just garden-variety anxiety. People get to this point, this fear, from many different paths. It's when we identify what's underneath the worry, identify our path(s), that we can understand what is influencing our barriers of *"I might need this someday,"* and why it becomes difficult to part with that item.

Do any of these sound like you?

- You grew up in a home that had very little, and you learned to scrimp, save, and make the most of *every*thing. You wasted nothing. Being wasteful feels like letting someone or those values down, and so you don't.

- You live like that now, because you have no other option

financially.

- You have a spouse or partner who feels this way, even if you don't. To have harmony in the home, you've ended up holding on to things, because you knew it would upset your other family member if you didn't. The need is not yours, but you honor the wishes of others.

- You've lived through loss, like a fire or a flood. You have fewer possessions because of it and cling to each of them more tightly.

- You're the kind of person who has received praise or pride from being a *"go-to"* person, a resourceful person, one who can help someone else in need by *"rescuing them"* when they don't have something, and this has become an important part of your identity. You hear yourself saying, *"I need to hold onto this, just in case someone else could use this and I can help them. That's the kind of person/friend family member/employee I want to be."*

- You're justifying the money you've already spent an on item, the sunk cost barrier we discussed: *"Well, the money I spent on this already is gone, so I should hold onto it so I can continue to justify the purchase with opportunities that MAY arise in the future."* This is the *"Bridesmaid Dress Syndrome,"* in which we are deluded into thinking we will get more use out of something in the future, thereby making the cost or the uniqueness easier to absorb in our minds.

- You're overstating the word *"need,"* and using it when you really mean *"want"* or *"could make use of this."* For example, I keep one t-shirt in my t-shirt collection that is a patriotic image, in case I want to wear something thematic on 4th of July. I created a need in my head, and I've decided this item will fill it. Of course, it's really a *want*, but I've promoted it to a need, because I've imagined a scenario in which this fits the bill.

- You're afraid that if you let go of something, and were put in a position later when you could have used that item, it will sting or embarrass. When this happens, it makes you feel like a failure, like you're letting people down, letting yourself down, when you're not perfectly prepared for what may come. *"I want to avoid a situation in which I'm not happy with myself in the future, so I'm willing to hold onto all this stuff to prevent such a situation."*

Any or many of these may resonate with you, or maybe there are even other reasons out there that you feel drive this fear in you. Whatever the reason, the underlying impact is that worried feeling, the one that causes the barrier to go up.

This worry causes stress, and considering letting go of things creates conflict between your desire to live a freer life and your fear that you will face a time in the future of regret, loss, waste, or failure. **Your desire to live with less stress some point in the future requires coexisting with much more stress until that point.** The barrier arises when you're willing to trade off today's stress for tomorrow: *"I'd rather deal with the very stressful life of stuff and clutter today, than face the potential stress of not being able to meet a need tomorrow."*

When this barrier comes up, it is important to know how easily it arrives, and that it can seem harmless for just one item, here or there. After a while, it turns into a room full of items that you've held onto, just on the chance you might need it someday. Recognize it when it comes up, and then face it with a rationale which helps put it in your current context of life. *"I know that I hold onto things out of worry for the future, but, I also know the negative side that comes from this activity. I feel overwhelmed, guilty about my spending, exhausted by the effort it takes to maintain and store items I will probably never use. THOSE are the feelings I want to erase, more so than the feeling of guilt or fear that I might need something someday."*

When these two sides come into conflict, your desire for a better life today vs. your fear of what may come tomorrow, who will win? ***Who do YOU root for today?***

One exercise that can help you see who you're rooting for is to understand your <u>ideal</u> portfolio of belongings. If you think about what the right ratio or percentages of things you keep in your life might be, what would you come up with?

> 1) **Memories of your past.** They have no practical value besides helping you reminisce about previous parts of your life.
>
> 2) **Things you need, love and use TODAY**, in your current lifestyle, and in the foreseeable future.
>
> 3) **Things you don't need or use right now**, and cannot honestly say for sure if you'll ever need them, but you're saving them, just in case.

What would the ideal percentages be? Is it 5% past, 90% current, 5% future? Some other ratio? Whatever your answer, make sure the math adds up to 100%. As you start to go through your things and make some decisions, notice the reality of what your percentages are today. You won't measure them exactly, but you'll have them in mind as you're looking around at what's staying in the "*keep*" pile, and noticing if the amounts are roughly in line with what you already said might be reasonable.

Does what you're keeping in your "*stuff portfolio*" match your ideal ratio? Or has it tipped into the past or future buckets more than you thought it should? When your reality is significantly different than what your ideal is, you know how strong the barriers of future fear or of sentimentality, which we tackle in the next chapter, really are. We know where the heaviest work for you to achieve your goal of how you want to live your life, and what kind of space you must dedicate to "*stuff*" will be.

Once you start to review your items with your ideal ratio and the resulting boundaries are established, decision-making comes down to an item-by-item review. There are many practical steps you can take when this barrier arises. The first is to ask yourself some specific questions that help bring focus to the "*I might need it someday*" barrier that comes up:

- "*Is this really a need? Or is it a want?*"
- "*What is the real probability that the 'someday' scenario will come about?*"
- "*What would I do if that scenario came about and I didn't have it? How would I move forward?*"

- "Is this something I could borrow? Rent? Substitute something else to do the job?" This is one of the most overlooked concepts as we think about our stuff: **What do we just need to ACCESS, but not OWN?**

- "Could I replace it easily and inexpensively enough if it turns out I do need it?" Some people use the "$20 and 20 minutes" rule -- if you could replace something for $20 or less, and in 20 minutes or less, you're better off taking the risk of letting it go and getting the space and sanity back.

- "What is the worst thing that will happen if I let go of this item?"

- "What will I _gain_ if I let go of this item?"

(*Note: Check out the Appendix for a helpful Clever Girl's Cheat Sheet to keep with you when you're running through your needs analysis.*)

After you go through your questions, you can experiment with a few things:

- What is a category of belongings that you're most willing to take risks with? Could you start getting comfortable by letting go within a low-risk category? An example might be letting go of extra kitchen eating utensils; there is very low risk that you'll really need them again in the future, and on the small chance you did, you'd have multiple ways to fill the need at that time.

- Can you put some items in a "*time capsule*," stored safely away, where they can be accessed in the event of "*need*", but they are not taking space nor contributing to your sense of overwhelm or chaos that you're facing now? This would be as simple as a box or bin in a basement or closet. You would put a date in your calendar for a few months out for you to revisit and make decisions.

Finally, part of changing your relationship to stuff and facing this barrier is to keep your awareness up for your tendency to squirrel away things for the future when _new_ items come your way. By reducing what comes into your home in the future, you can make changes in your lifestyle by acquiring less, and let the inflow of new things become more manageable. It means recognizing that impulse-buys, the freebies and the hand-me-downs, and the gifts that come our way can all trigger the *"I might need this someday"* barrier. Facing it before it settles in somewhere in your home can be an enormous help for you to maintain how you want to live in your home.

If I'm fully honest, you may let go of something that, in the future, you could have used. You will remember you had it and you parted with it. If you let go of one hundred items, you'll regret 2 or 3 of them. A moment will come up, and you will say, *"Ugh! I had that, and I got rid of it!"* You may be upset with yourself, because you'll be in a moment and say to yourself *"I could have been more prepared for this than I am right now."* What you will also likely discover quickly is that what you needed can be is replaceable, accessible elsewhere, borrowable, or substitutable, or that your need for it isn't as strong as you really think it is. **Let's also keep in mind that there was also a good chance you wouldn't even have FOUND the item you needed when you looked for it, even if you** *"know it's around here, somewhere..."*

But between now and that moment, you'll be living a more peaceful, more enjoyable life, in the home you've created around your goals for how you live. The moment of regret? It may sting, but it is fleeting. And, you may never even notice all the stress and regret you DON'T have after letting go of all these things, things you will never ever think of again. The absence of regret will show up in your life simply as relief and peace.

Chapter VI: Sentimentality

> *"This reminds me of the time..."*
>
> *"This reminds me of someone..."*
>
> *"I wouldn't want to forget this..."*

Sentimental keepsakes, mementos, and memorabilia. We all have them. The **sentimentality** barrier comes up when we know we must reduce the keepsakes, but the emotional hold each piece has on us just won't allow us to do so. It's one of the toughest categories that I go through with clients. If you're reading this book, there's a good chance it's a tough one for you, too.

Keepsakes are items that, **without** the memory we've attached to them, *have no magic value beyond the original purpose of the item itself.* To most other people, they'd be meaningless. However, to us they've become treasured because we've associated a memory or importance to an otherwise unmemorable or unimportant item. Keepsakes come in many forms:

Ticket stubs, stuffed animals, a baby's outfits, graduation tassels, programs, buttons, figurines, T-shirts, jewelry, hats, bronzed shoes, trophies, pressed flowers, greeting cards, handmade cards from kids, toys, newspaper clippings, love letters, mix tapes, travel souvenirs, report cards, blankets, kids' artwork, matchbooks, shells and stones, baby teeth and hair, journals, foreign currency, books, school papers, sports memorabilia, china, yearbooks, old IDs, old planners or calendars, photos, postcards, and so on, and so on.

These items can be from our youth, from our former (and current) romances, our friends, our college days, our careers, our travels, or handed down from our family members to treasure. They are mementos from people who have left our lives or passed away, tokens of their identity and our relationship with them.

They are from great moments, or sad moments, or even from a moment that wasn't very special, but the way we remember it is. They're from moments that, at the time we said, *"I want to mark this occasion, and I'm going to hold onto this item to do so."*

Our collections and our hobbies, the leisure pursuits we've enjoyed over the years, can be keepsakes and memorabilia. Collections have been built not only in our hunt and search for treasure, but with gifts others have thoughtfully added to our collection, even if we weren't actively growing it ourselves.

Keepsakes and memorabilia can be everywhere, but their mere existence isn't a problem. So, when do sentimental items become a problem?

We love the emotions we feel when we touch and revisit them. Our hearts warm and we sigh for the past. We can get lost in our memorabilia for hours! But there can be a point where we know that we are just holding on to too much of it. Maybe it's driven by space needs, or just knowing how much is around us that is weighing us down. It could be preventing us from moving on after a loss or after a change in life. We may even address these things because we just don't want our loved ones to have to deal with all this stuff after we're gone. It can also come after going through the *"ideal ratio"* exercise discussed in the Future Fear chapter, and realizing that the ideal ratio and the reality are just way out of sync.

If we have a goal of reducing what we have, and our sentimental items are part of it, we get there by saying to ourselves, *"I enjoy the memory that this item conjures up for me. But I can live without it, especially if it helps me get to my bigger goals for my life now. I can let go of this."*

It is when we can't bring ourselves to say that statement, when we just can't let those items leave our lives, that we recognize our barrier is going up, and it is preventing us from letting go.

At first, the barrier feels like a general unwillingness, and it can be strong enough to not look past it. However, the barrier, deep down, once again, is usually **fear**:

- We are afraid of feeling like we'll lose part of ourselves if we part with an item.
- We fear the thought of parting with those items, as if we're either betraying our past self, or someone else.
- We are afraid we'll lose the memory itself, and our ability to revisit or share our story, without it.

- We believe we'll want to continue to revisit these emotions time and time again, and fear that, without this keepsake to hold in our hands, we won't be able to recapture the joy. Not being able to recapture joy seems like something to avoid!

All of those scenarios, those emotions, we tend to want to avoid. Forever.

We all love our collections and our walks down memory lane and should have some keepsakes for our ability to do that. I'm not suggesting that we shouldn't hold onto meaningful things. Think about your goals and decide whether holding on to too many items that have little or no other value besides *"triggers old memory"* take up more of your home than you feel they should, given how you want to live in the space.

I will walk you through a few steps to the process of reviewing and downsizing your collection of keepsakes and memorabilia, and I will guide you by giving you some questions you can ask yourself as you go through the process.

First, since we're talking about the sentimental, and not the practical, we need some *"big picture"* philosophical questions to help guide you through it and help you understand the role each item plays in your life. These are meant to help you see the difference between items being *memorable* and items being *important*. Just because something triggers a memory doesn't mean it is also important to you.

As you think critically about items, ask:

- What do you gain from keeping this? What do you lose from keeping it?

- What do you gain from letting it go? What do you lose from letting it go?

- What would your past-self say if it knew you still had this, and what would your future-self say if it knew you let go of it?

- Are you keeping it <u>primarily</u> because you want someone else (child, grandchild, etc.) to find it as emotionally valuable as you do, maybe even after you're gone? (kids' artwork and old report cards, anyone?) And, do you know for sure they will value it as you hope they will? (We're going to talk about this again in Chapter VII "Perceived Value to Someone Else," too.)

- Are the memories and the keepsake even yours, or are they the memories of someone else, that have ended up in your hands through gift or inheritance? Is the *item* important to you, or is that *person* important?

- Does the item bring you sadness or make you feel bad about yourself or someone else? Sometimes, our memorabilia bring up negative feelings: guilt, sadness, regret, heartbreak. Yet, for whatever reason, we still feel committed to holding onto these things to rekindle the memories of our life's experience. Is holding onto things that bring about negative feelings really a good thing for you and your home?

- Are you keeping it because someone else expects you to, but it doesn't mean much to you, personally? In other words, is the primary emotion you attach to it <u>obligation or guilt</u>?

- If someone you care about accidentally came across this item, would it be awkward or upsetting to them?

- Do you really know WHY it is so important to you? Are you just accepting an easy, on-the-surface answer, or is there a deeper meaning behind your attachment to this, and you're not facing it?

Okay, they don't ALL have to be big and heavy questions. There are some <u>practical questions</u> we can ask, too:

- How much space of your very valuable real estate and storage space are you willing to allocate to items that don't have a function, but only serve to generate memories when you revisit them? Can you set a limit to the space, and then prioritize what ends up in that space?

- Do you have more than one item that reminds you of that

person, place, or moment? Would you be okay if you kept only one or a small set of those items? This comes up so often when going through things like children's old clothing or artwork. I know how tough this is; be disciplined with yourself with this!

Do you need ten outfits from when your child was growing up, to help you remember they were that age once, especially if you have a picture of your child wearing it? Do you need every rainbow picture that was finger painted?

- Can you rank importance among them? Set up four piles, and rank what goes in each:

    – *"I could never, ever, ever let go of this item, and if the house caught fire, I'd rescue it."*

    – *"I am glad I've kept this. I enjoy revisiting it occasionally, if I stumble upon it. If it were gone forever, I'd miss it, but it wouldn't really impact my life."*

    – *"Hmm, I kept it at the time, but I don't need it anymore. Sure, I remember a moment when I look at it, but it's not a critical part of how my life has turned out."*

    – *"Honestly, I have no idea why I kept this in the first place."*

- Do you need to keep the item as it is, or could you take a photo of it? Scan copies of cards or letters? Create a digital scrapbook? Capture it all in a cloud-based collection of images or videos that you can keep for yourself or share with others electronically? Or turn into a collection in a shadow box? Or a keepsake quilt? Do you need the whole item, like the program from the school musical you were in, or could you edit it down to just the parts that are meaningful?

- Do you truly have the space to store and display your collection at its current volume? Has your collection taken over space that would be more valuable if used in a different way?

- Are you able to appreciate the collection with how much you

have, or have the special pieces been lost in the numbers?
- Is there someone else who'd love to have the keepsake for their own memories? This is a good way to think about family heirlooms... you may have other family that would love them, too.

As you walk through these questions, you should start to feel a difference between what you can let go of and what you won't. It gets easier over time, as you become stronger at finding the clarity in what is important for your future, and not just evidence of your past. It can also get easier over time, if the pressure to reduce your possessions means you need to make deeper cuts into what you're keeping. When you have no choice, you stop allowing yourself to choose.

Part II has a chapter specifically on some how-to when focusing on reducing your memorabilia or collections so I won't focus on it here. If you were to walk away with three important ideas about managing your keepsakes and memories, I hope they would be:

- Write your stories down. Not only does this help you capture your memories, but it helps share them with others and pass on the stories after you're no longer able to tell people about what is important to you and why.
- Honor what you're keeping. If your keepsakes are in a box in the basement or attic and you never look at them, what value are they really playing in your life? If items are important to you and bring you happiness, can you make them more prominent in your life? If something is not important enough to be featured prominently, are you questioning why you are holding on to it?
- Remember that our stuff is *stuff*. It is not our memories. It is not the people we love. Our memories are in our heads and our hearts. Keep this idea in mind when we address the "*how*" of letting go of memorabilia in Part II.

Chapter VII: Perceived Value To Someone Else

"My kids might want this."

*"My kids will want this,
even though they now think that they won't."*

"I could give this as a gift to someone someday."

*"This will help people be reminded of me and
feel connected to me when I'm gone."*

"I'm sure somebody could use this."

This can be a very common challenge for people, and it has multiple levels, which makes it even tougher. The first is the nature of the barrier itself, in which you're holding onto things because you **perceive they have value to someone else**, but you're not able to accept that this may not be true. The second is the reaction that can come after you accept it to be true.

A reason this one can be so difficult is that this intention often, though not exclusively, comes from a very good place, where you are well-meaning, thoughtful and generous. This can be a strong and powerful desire, and when you want to be generous, you want to and find a way in which someone benefits from that. It can be for someone you already know, such as your children or other relatives, or for someone you don't, such as finding a needy and deserving family who will want your possessions. You're willing to give someone something you own for free.

It can also come from a desire to serve a legacy you have built during your life, and have that legacy be honored by others. In cases of heirlooms, antiques, items shared and passed down through the family, there is a sense of duty to pass it to someone else someday, and to believe that the intended receiver will accept it with the same honor and duty that you feel.

Your own personal attachment of value to an item, and your assumption that others will appreciate and value it in the same way might also create this desire to hold onto things. The example of saving the kids' artwork and report cards comes to mind: You feel strongly that your children will want these items to look back on, and you feel a sense of duty to preserve these items for them. You believe they will feel the importance in the items just as much as you do.

Perhaps these thoughts arrive as one step beyond the purposeless practicality barrier. You acknowledged, *"This is still good, but I'm ready to let it go."* You might be invested in passing it along because of what something is worth, based on what you've paid for it or the quality of the item, and your belief that this value and quality should live on with others after you're done with it.

So, when do these thoughts start to become a barrier?

The barrier is created when these aspirations and intentions *aren't* matching with the reality of the situation, and yet you're still committed to the idea. It arrives when you learn a response to your expectations that you just don't want to hear, but you don't accept it as the end of your options or are in disbelief:

- The people you hope will want the items do not want them.
- The quality of an item isn't seen as high to others as you think it is, or the market value of the item isn't what you imagined it is.
- Other people don't hold importance in an item in the same way you have.
- You're stuck on the concept of wanting to find a potential recipient, but don't know whom that might be or how you might find that person.

When you are hearing that there isn't a market for giving something away for free, as a gift or donation, and yet you're still holding onto these items with hopes that this reality will change, your barrier is up.

As I said earlier, the second challenge is what can come after you acknowledge the barrier: In learning that reality doesn't match our expectations, our feelings can be very hurt.

If it turns out the answer is, *"No, I don't want it,"* or, *"No, no one wants it,"* or even, *"No, this isn't good enough to donate, and it is probably trash,"* it can feel like personal rejection. It isn't just that your stuff has been rejected. YOU can feel rejected. Your taste. Choices you've made. How you've spent your money. What made you happy. What you'd consider acceptable. When you find that others don't feel the same way, it can really sting. And it can be hard not to take it personally.

So how do we break down this barrier and move forward from the emotional impact it creates?

There are four steps to take to leap past the barriers:

> 1) Understand that when people or organizations do not want your possessions, it's not personal. *You* are not being rejected.
>
> 2) Accept how society has and continues to change; people value different things today than they used to value.
>
> 3) Consider the intended recipient's mindset and respect it, in the same way that you'd like yours to be respected. Your children may have different styles and tastes, or different goals for how they want to live in their own home. They may be struggling with clutter in the same way you are, and adding more feels like moving backward for them.
>
> 4) Utilize strategies that help you take real action.
>
>> - If your child doesn't want something of good quality, can you come up with another destination for it?
>>
>> - If you're struggling with where something could go, can you be creative about the profile of the kind of person who might appreciate it? This may help others find a destination for you. (Example: instead of *"A musician for those old records,"* try to find *"Someone who appreciates the early jazz period and owns a record player."*)
>>
>> - If the answer is that the items aren't suitable for charitable donation, can you find other beneficiaries for your goods, like people who will use them for something else completely differently?
>>
>> - Can you work with a junk removal company who

works aggressively to recycle everything possible?

These action steps are geared towards continuing to support your decision-making, your evaluation of the reality of the market or recipients, and your ability to let things go and really have them go.

It can be disappointing not to have your items go to where or whom you imagined they might. It is helpful to remember, however, that **you** loved, used, and enjoyed the items. You can reflect on the fact that what has been most important to you have not been things, but your memories, relationships, achievements, triumphs over struggle, and the impact you've had on the lives of others around you. What has been most important to you has never, ever, been your stuff.

CHAPTER VIII: WANT TO DISPOSE OF SAFELY OR SMARTLY

"I don't want it to go to a landfill."

*"I don't want to just waste it.
I could turn it into something else."*

*"I'm don't know how to get rid of this properly,
and I'm afraid of something bad will happen."*

Like many of the barriers in this book, this comes from a well-meaning place. This one has its roots in a sense of responsibility and risk management, two of my favorite qualities in a person. Whether it is a responsibility towards the environment or a sense of risk management of the downsides of irresponsible disposal, this one has its foundation in values, ethics, and duty.

A barrier gets created, however, when someone's sense of duty to that responsibility becomes the *sole* reason to hold onto an item that would otherwise leave the home, and prevents the person from living life as he or she intends. The item no longer serves any purpose and the owner truly no longer wants it there, but there is no feasible or immediately visible exit strategy. The barrier is to the actual action of the exit, not the decision making of whether or not the item is worth keeping. When you want to **dispose of something smartly or safely**, but your inability to make that happen means you're holding onto items indefinitely, the barrier is created. Over time, and in extreme cases, the number of items that can be harbored can start to overwhelm a space. (*Note: I'm not speaking here about hoarding disorder, the definition of which is the persistent difficulty discarding or parting with possessions, regardless of their actual value. I'm referring to people who have truly determined that the item can be let go, and even disposed of without going to a new owner.*)

When you have the space and time to have the quality of life in your home that you desire, it isn't creating a problem. So, when does it become a problem? When you are sacrificing your quality of life in your home because you have more "*someday*" projects, and not enough room for what you need, want and use now, it is a problem. When you've allocated an amount of stuff and storage to your "*someday*" projects, but your time and ability to complete those projects will *never* match your supply, it is a problem. When *other* people in your home feel that they are suffering because of it, even if it doesn't feel like suffering to you, it is a problem.

As you come around to addressing the problem, however, and begin to make shifts in your priorities about what you are keeping and why you are keeping it, the barrier can start to appear. The barrier is the paralyzing conflict between your resistance to letting go of things in a way that feels irresponsible, and your goal of living with less stuff, less clutter, less stress.

The desire to keep things out of a landfill can put you in a position of just surrendering to keep it, indefinitely. It can start as one item here, another one there. As these piles grow in your home, you can see how trying to save the planet, one rescued item at a time, can lead to an impact in your own home that can feel just as wasteful. Your valuable real estate and storage space are being occupied by items you no longer value, but just can't seem to abandon. You have become willing to dedicate space in your home to this delayed decision because you just don't want to face reality. Some things are just going to be trash, either because you don't have another option, or are tired of waiting for another option to magically arrive.

There are three types of *"holding on past the point of having value"* patterns that can grow to cause problems to grow in your home, and wrestling them brings up the barrier of feeling conflicted with your values:

- Responsible recycling,
- Potential for upcycling, and
- Concerns about risk and vulnerability.

Responsible recycling: Imagine if you felt that you MUST recycle every piece of paper that came your way, but there was no recycling option within 50 miles of you. What would that pile of paper in your home look like? I'm exaggerating, but the piles *can* add up.

Even when proper disposable is available, without an action plan and taking action, it can begin to overwhelm. For instance, it's great that your town has a hazardous waste day once a year, but if you're never bringing things to the collection, you're not utilizing the disposal options available. The pile grows, for yet another year, because you don't want to just throw it in the trash. So, the waste is yours to harbor.

If you neither have an easy path to pursue, or you don't seem to be pursuing the path available, yet you are committed to recycling the items, this can develop into a problem.

Potential for upcycling. Another way in which this problem can develop is in the resistance to letting go of something, because it seems wasteful or harmful to do so, and committing instead to give it new life. This is repurposing or *"upcycling,"* in which an item which has lost its value in its original form can be turned into something else. Until it is upcycled, it doesn't have value in its current form; it only has *potential*.

One step deeper is when someone stops by the side of the road to take someone else's discards to turn into something else or to say that it can be used. This goes further than being responsible for your own possessions, and instead taking on the burden created by others.

Even the finished upcycling projects can have different depths of value. Sometimes, an item can be turned into something very useful, useful right now, by a particular person. *"Mom has been looking for a new way to organize her cutting boards, and this rack can be just the thing to do it."* Sometimes, it's just an interesting thing someone saw on the internet and thought they'd try. Turning an antique milk can into an umbrella stand can be interesting and functional. Turning and old milk can into an umbrella stand when you only use collapsible umbrellas or live in a desert is just a fun art project, turning one no-longer-used item into another won't-be-used-either item.

As an activity or a hobby, this isn't necessarily a problem. People are often drawn to an item and say, *"I could make this thing out of that old thing or that piece of trash."* It can be a good thing for the environment, creative, and fun. However, when your home is full of items that would otherwise be tossed, and your dream of turning them into something else isn't matched with your time, your skills, or your energy, it can be a problem.

Concerns about risk and vulnerability. The other part of this responsibility barrier is the risk management side. There are times that you've absolutely decided to let something go, and you wish you could, but the exit strategy seems elusive or complicated.

In this situation, a person wants to get rid of something, but believes there is a right way and a wrong way. The person may know the right way, but does not know how to access it. As a result, rather than do the *"wrong"* thing, he does nothing. The item sits, out of the way, but maybe not, and is a monument of inaction.

Some examples of the situations:

- **Prescription drugs and prescription bottles.** People tend to have an awareness that they shouldn't be careless about prescription drugs. However, what to do with them tends to be confusing. All sorts of home-based methods can come up as options, but then you hear *"don't do that"* or *"do this instead"* and it can be confusing. Throw them away? Flush them? Mix them with coffee grounds? Bring them to the police or the doctor? People don't want to do the wrong thing. Contact the pharmacy or police department to ask what local resources exist. Many towns have regularly established collection processes for prescription drugs and sharps. While the bottles themselves aren't dangerous, they have personal information on them that you might not want out in the recycling at the curb, either. Removing labels or blocking text on labels can help with that.

- **Hazardous waste.** This is another situation where you know you want it out of your home, but also know that you shouldn't just throw it in the trash, because it can be dangerous for others. Again, many people know what their local hazardous waste collection support is; check with your local department of public works. Even locations that have these services can be limited to *"but we don't take this"* or *"we only do it one day a year."* There is no doubt that this can feel like a big barrier to action.

- **Personally Identifiable Information (PII)**. When dealing with papers, there are so many sources of personally identifiable information, the stuff you wouldn't want in the hands of identity thieves. From tax forms and pay stubs even to addresses on magazines and labels on junk mail, there can be information out there that, in the wrong hands, can pose a danger. Anything that has a signature, social security number, legal or medical information, account number, or appears to be offering you credit is something which would go in this category. Many of us know this, and have well-intentioned shred piles or rip things up. But eventually, the shred pile grows. It gets too large to imagine shredding yourself. You then think you might bring them somewhere, but don't know where you can go that you'd trust. You start to dream about just putting it all in the fireplace, but wonder if that would just create a fiery mess. Back to square one: *"What do I do with all this?"*

- **Computers and the equipment that have personal information on it.** People are smart enough to know they don't want to pass along an item without clearing off all your personal information. However, this can be a challenge for people who don't have the technological know-how or are aware of the resources available to help accomplish this. So, they save a stack of laptops, a box of old desktops, a drawer with old phones, because they either don't know the right way of dealing with it, or it feels to be more effort than they want to make to see it through.

- **Religious relics.** Whether someone is devout or not, there can be a sense of responsibility that is associated with disposing of blessed or holy items. More and more, however, churches or synagogues, etc. don't have the space to just take items from people. People don't want the items to get in the wrong hands, so they end up holding onto them, even though in their mind, they've decided they'd let go of them if they could.

Again, the desire to be responsible and not impact the world negatively is an important value for many of us. It is when our commitment to that value and our desire to live differently in our homes comes into conflict that the barrier appears. There are many ways to explore options for resolving some of these issues created by the desire to keep thing out of a landfill or have their disposal leaving you feeling vulnerable.

1) Researching a destination or method is step one. Research local options for solving these issues. Many of these issues have been faced by others around you; how have they addressed it? Break the task down into manageable steps.

2) Preparing your items for disposal is step two. Executing on disposal is step three. Rather than be overwhelmed with the whole process, make the tasks discreet and achievable.

3) Recognize that spending some money on a solution may help resolve this. If you're looking for free resources, you may need to search longer. There will be options for things like shredding, computer disposal, and some hazardous waste items that may require a fee.

4) Understand that some of this requires settling the conflict that exists in your head about the issue. It can be hard to find fault in the well-intended resistance. Here's the tough part: If you're committed to this responsibility, and truly can't find a solution that meets your needs perfectly, only a couple of options remain:

– **Compromise on your values.** When you're facing this barrier, you have competing goals: *"The feeling I'm trying to achieve for my home and life"* vs. *"I have a responsibility to protect the environment and prevent dangerous outcomes."* There are times when you cannot choose both, and you must compromise yourself to move forward.

– Surrender to the idea that **you are essentially renting out your home to the landfill**, and you're just putting off an inevitable action. If you are too afraid of letting things leave your home purely because you don't want them to end up in a landfill, you have created permanent space in your home for items you've already deemed to be *worthless*. At some point in time, you, or someone after you, *will* need to deal with these items.

These can both sound like awful solutions, and neither of them feels very solution-y. There are steps you can take to help wrestle with this very difficult challenge.

- Value yourself and your home as much as you value the earth. Don't let YOUR home become the landfill.

- Recognize that all your values may not be achievable in the same way or at the same time in life. Revisit your bigger picture here: What is your <u>real</u> goal right now?

- Research and hunt down answers. Give items away for free to someone else who might make use of them in ways you just won't, just to get it out of your home.

- Consider a threshold of a percentage you can accept: *"I really tried, but it is unavoidable. I've done so well with so many other things, but I'm going to have to miss on these items."*

Ultimately, confronting this barrier is about making peace with your actions, as you serve both your goals for how you want to live in your home and your sense of responsibility. We can't all be perfect, all the time, and that can be very humbling. It does not, however, have to paralyze us from progress in life.

PART II

How to Tackle Five Tough Categories

Part II: How to Tackle Five Tough Categories

In Part I, we dove deep into exploring *"why"* you hold onto things. There were eight common points of resistance, and you may have identified with one or many of them. The perspective on understanding your *"why"* is the first step. It helps prepare your readiness for change. Turning that into a new approach to action, your *"how,"* is where change genuinely occurs.

Part II provides a structure or a playbook for how to approach and tackle five of the most common areas of struggle. These categories can grow to be overwhelming, and many of your barriers can appear when you face them and review what you own and why you own it:

- Clothes
- Books
- Collections/Memorabilia
- Photos
- Paperwork

You have probably struggled with editing at least one of these categories. Editing is just like you might think of in writing; you review what is there as a whole or bit-by-bit, and make decisions about what should stay, what can go, in order for the end result to be a great one. It is the same thing with your categories of stuff.

Before you start any editing project, however, I want you to set yourself up for success. If you're interested in going through your possessions and letting go of items, but you're dreading it or fear you won't be able to accomplish as much as you want (or, as much as someone else may be expecting of you), make sure you're doing all you can to support yourself BEFORE you get to the hard part. Here are 10 steps to take; any or all will help you as you move into tackling your goals:

1) **Set a vision.** What do you hope to accomplish? What will it look like when you are done?

2) **Write your goals.** Have your goals written, so you know what

you are hoping to achieve, and you can use them to guide your plan.

3) **Know your *"why,"* your motivation for doing all of this.** When you know exactly WHY you are working towards letting things go, it will help keep you grounded and focused as you move through your more challenging moments.

4) **Be accountable to someone else.** Being accountable to someone else helps people stay on track when it comes to keeping important goals. It's harder to give up when you know someone else is watching! Let someone else know you're trying to achieve these goals and give them permission to check in to see how things are going, or you volunteer to self-report on your progress.

5) **Pace Yourself.** You don't want to get burned out. This goes for both physical and mental energy. When dealing with tough decisions, there is such a thing as *"decision fatigue,"* where you start to make less effective decisions because you're too tired to think or too weak to even argue with yourself anymore. Pace yourself in terms of time you spend. Take short breaks (but don't get distracted!), get fresh air, and stay fed and hydrated.

6) **Get to the honest answers, whenever you can.** It's going to be really easy to talk yourself out of letting go of things; if it weren't, you'd be done by now! Ask yourself the tough questions, and keep in mind your goals and your *"why"* answers. Keep *"purposeful possession"* in mind: *"do I really have a good reason to keep this?"* Be honest with yourself.

7) **Have the right tools.** Sometimes, success comes down to having the right tools when you start the job. Not having tools in place can be a delay: a reason to get distracted, a reason to not finish a project, a reason to stay disorganized. Think through and assemble what you need before you start. This could be boxes or bags for taking things away from your home. It could include anticipating the different piles you will create while sorting, maybe even having labels for those to help you keep track. It could be a marker and a pack of sticky notes. You get the idea. Gather your tools before you start, and you'll have a better chance of avoiding

distractions and following through.

8) **Start small and follow through.** For some people, it is not the starting of the project that is hard; it's the *finishing* that's tough. The whole point of this book is about exploring those barriers that get in your way, psychologically and emotionally, but there are other hindrances that will come up along the way. Not enough time. Not enough space. Not enough support from other people in your home who get frustrated by the "*it gets worse before it gets better*" phenomenon of decluttering. Whether your barriers are the ones in this book or just the reality of life around you, working hard to stay focused, follow through, and finish is a big key to your success. The easiest way to get on the right track is START SMALL. It is easy to get overwhelmed when your goal is "*Clean out closet.*" Set measurable and specific goals, like, "*Go through sock drawer and eliminate the ones I don't love and don't wear often. Donate those to the homeless shelter in town.*" When your goal is something you can see and you can build a plan around, it is easier to follow through.

9) **Celebrate your accomplishments and learn from your successes.** Getting organized is not just a finish line. Organizing is an ongoing process, constantly making progress towards new goals, with new effort and accomplishments. As a result, not only is it tough to feel "*finished*," it's even tougher to feel the freedom to feel good about what has been accomplished and truly acknowledge it and celebrate. A day that is better than yesterday is a day worth celebrating. A day with fewer arguments or less stress, because of the organization or the habit changes you've implemented is a day worth celebrating. Change is hard; take the time to recognize your hard work, your progress, and pat yourself on the back.

Evaluating how the process went so that you can think about what was harder than you thought, what was easier, what went well, what you'd change for the next project you tackle, is a great way to increase the productivity you have on these kinds of projects.

10) **Be kinder to yourself than you are to your stuff.** It's an interesting point of view, isn't it? It's one we don't think about

much. When we're valuing our stuff over the quality of our own lives, when we're holding onto to things, despite the stress and overwhelm that they cause, we're being kinder to our stuff than we are to ourselves. Maybe it's time we change that.

This process may even take a few rounds. Your first round may find some easy decisions, the obvious *"toss"* items. A few rounds later, after you've lived with your decisions, or moved on to other categories, you'll benefit from a broadened perspective of what you truly value, love, and use. You may find that letting go of things, and getting stronger at decision-making, leads to a feeling of contagious decluttering! Like any other tough exercise, sometimes we start off more slowly before we build those muscles and find that groove. Don't be afraid to say, *"This was a good first round, and I'm going to come back again in a couple of days or weeks for round two."* Just be sure to actually *do* that.

With that, let's march into those challenging areas, shall we?

Chapter I: Clothing

The need or desire to pare down a wardrobe can come from many reasons, including: struggling with limited space, the desire to sell some items to generate income, or the realization that the sheer volume of clothing actually prevent you from finding the clothes you want to wear, when you want to wear them.

Even with the best intentions for the positives that this project can bring, many barriers may still come up. Here are just a few that come to mind:

Future Fear: *"I've been a bunch of sizes. I can't predict what I'll need. I'm afraid I won't have anything to wear if I get to that size again."* Or *"But, what if I have to go to a fancy event someday, and need a gown to wear?"*

Purposeless Practicality: *"This shirt is still in good shape (even though I never wear it)"* or, *"I used to wear suits all the time for my job"* or, *"I thought for sure I'd lose that weight…"*

Sunk Cost: *"This dress was really expensive (though, I never wear it)."*

Recoup the Cost: *"This is a designer label. Someone will buy this from me."*

Guilt: *"My brother bought this for me. I never really loved it, but it would hurt his feelings if I got rid of this."*

Perceived value to someone else: *"My sister might like this. I'll hold onto it and ask her."*

And even:

Sentimentality: *"I wore this on my first date with my husband."*

One closet can hold all these barriers for the same person at once. No wonder reviewing and editing our wardrobes can be so overwhelming!

This is one of the most common categories of *"stuff"* I help clients with all the time. A process I use for projects like this one is my **EEEEZ** method:

- **Excavate**: remove of most or all things, even just one category at a time, to see everything you own.
- **Evaluate**: engage in critical thinking and set up guidelines

around what you need and what can go.

- **Edit**: follow those guidelines, piece by piece, to select the items that stay and the items that leave.
- **Establish Zones**: create a system and flow for storage and retrieval of items that make sense for the space you have, and for the items you're keeping.

We start with **Excavate**.

You're going to find and gather the clothes in your closet, your dresser, your armoire, wherever they are. The goal is to remove everything, and layout in a place you can work, but the process may involve sections or stages. With clothes, it is often good to start with one category: sweaters, T-shirts, underwear, etc. It may mean bringing them out from different places you have them stashed, so that you can see everything. You can also just work shelf by shelf, drawer by drawer, if that feels like the more manageable way to work through your space, or you don't have a large spot you can lay things out to review.

Sort and group the items in a way that will be meaningful for your decision-making. For instance, you may be working on t-shirts and want to separate out *"t-shirts I can wear to work"* vs. *"t-shirts I'd never wear to work."* Socks may be: athletic socks, dress socks, novelty socks, etc. You may also group by color; this can be very helpful if you happen to be drawn to the same types of clothing, over and over. For many people, black may be the most common color of shirts or dresses. Grouping them together allows you to see the full collection and make comparisons as you evaluate.

For **Evaluate**, you'll set the guidelines or rules you'll use for making decisions. Some people are going to have a "gut" feeling about things and don't need criteria. If that sounds like you, and you're making progress towards your goals by knowing that how you feel about an item is enough, then that may be all the guidelines you need. For some, however, logic and criteria are necessary.

Regardless of using feeling or criteria, some basic ground rules apply:

- The clothes you keep all fit you now, or are one size up or down, and a realistic fit for the near future. Sizes outside of that range should be removed from your wardrobe, and then either donated/sold (top choice) or bagged/boxed up and put somewhere else as space permits, so they are not getting in the way of you having a fully functioning wardrobe and choices each day.

- They are not stained, torn, or damaged, unless they're clothes you set aside for things like painting, lawn mowing, or playing football in the mud.
- The clothes are yours to decide what to do with, or they're someone else's you have full authority or permission to review. For instance, you may not have your spouse's permission to just go through his or her stuff on your own, but you might be responsible for that of your young children or tweens without them even being in the room.

From there, you can set up some guidelines and decision-making criteria for evaluation. You can develop your own guidelines, or use my simple, *"five rules"* approach. With this approach, here are questions you can ask yourself about each piece and some examples of how you'll know your answer:

1) *"Do I love it?"*

    - You love how you look and feel when you wear it.
    - When you think of something you want to wear on any given day, it's high in the rotation, on the top of your list.
    - When you put it on, you tend to keep it on, rather than change your mind and change into something else.

2) *"Does it love me back?"*

    - It flatters your current shape.
    - It feels comfortable when you sit, stand, or walk while wearing it.

- It doesn't itch or have scratchy seams.
- You feel comfortable with the neckline, waist height, leg length, sleeve length, etc.
- You don't get distracted by it during the day when you're wearing it, worried whether it still looks okay.
- The color works with your complexion.
- If you ran into someone you once dated while you were wearing it, you would feel comfortable being seen wearing it.

3) *"Does it fit my current and foreseeable lifestyle?"*

- It fits into your normal current lifestyle: work clothing appropriate for your current job, casual clothing, or special occasions that are likely to occur. Some questions to figure that out:

– Special occasion clothing – if it is an *"I can wear this to a wedding"* item, is it one you WILL wear, or just COULD wear? Do you tend to wear repeats, or shop for something new each time?

– Special occasion clothing – *"This is good for a holiday party"* — how often do you normally attend these types of parties, and is it likely you'll wear this item at that time?

– Work clothing — especially suits or formal business clothing — do you wear these for your job now? Is it highly likely you'll wear them in the future? If yes, are THESE the suits you'll wear at that time?

– Casual clothing — do you have a lifestyle that you have enough opportunity to wear the casual clothing you have? Some examples: Eight great *"hang out in a ski lodge"* sweaters, but you only go skiing once a year? Five very-worn tops good for painting or a messy chore, but you're not really painting or doing *"dirty work"* that requires that many wardrobe options? The supply of these clothes is greater than the demand for them in your life.

– Accessories – yes, the item *could* go with particular outfits, but *do* you wear it? Do you still own the outfit that the accessory was originally intended to match?

- You have the right amount of what you need for core items (example: jeans, black pants, white or blue dress shirts, etc.). If you wear black pants every day, what is the realistic amount to have on hand, and how does that compare to the size of your collection? If your collection is greater, how do you prioritize on any given day what you choose to wear? Use the same guideline when deciding how many you choose to keep.

- The care this item requires fits easily into your lifestyle. You don't want all the hand-wash-only and dry-clean-only items to end up in a pile, worn once, left to die a lonely death of cashmere, silk, linen, and sequins. If it is dry clean only, or hand wash, or some care that just isn't part of your life right now, the maintenance required to keep it may be more than the item is worth to you.

4) *"If I went shopping today, would I pick it out and buy it?"*

If you went shopping today, and saw it, you would definitely pick it out and buy it. If that isn't true, if you wouldn't pick it out to buy today, why do you think you'd actually <u>wear</u> this tomorrow? Sure, we all have clothes that we bought when we were shopping for something (or nothing) specific. It may have served its purpose in our life. If it's not something you'd make the same choice to take home today, why are you KEEPING it in your home?

5) *"Am I realistically getting more use out of this than someone else could?"*

It is a *"yes"* to all the previous questions, and you do *actually wear* it. If you don't, it may be a good piece that looks good on you, that you like, and can imagine wearing it someday, but if you are not wearing it, it may mean you aren't really valuing it. Could someone else use it and love it so much that it is the *top of their list* of things they own?

Winter coats are a good example of this. You may have several perfectly great coats, but more than you know you need. Someone else really, really, really needs one, and would be grateful for yours. Business suits are another example, for people who don't have good clothing to wear to job interviews. Or shoes. And so on, and so on, and so on.

After setting your guidelines for decision-making, the next step is to apply them as you **Edit**. You'll go through your clothing, piece by piece, and, when you're stumped or you feel resistance or a barrier showing up, test it with the evaluate questions and guidelines.

This process can start slowly, but you will get the hang of it. As you do, you will make better decisions when you go through your categories. You may find some categories are easy and some are more challenging. Keep with it! Break the project up as you need to. This helps you avoid both overwhelm and a bedroom that looks like a war zone when you no longer have the energy to continue. It can be very helpful at this point to remove the items that aren't staying from the space in which you're working. If you can remove them from your home, that's even better!

Once you've completed your editing, it is on to setting up your new system! The goal is to design a system that supports access, ease of decision-making, and ease of maintenance and productivity. You'll **Establish Zones** that work for your space and your belongings. What is the easiest spot to access? That should probably hold your most frequently accessed items. For most people, your prime or most ideal zone for storage will be spaces between your shoulder height and your knee height; these are the most convenient for you to reach. Items you only use occasionally can be moved a bit further out of your prime zones.

Whether you're setting up your closet or reestablishing how you use your dresser drawers, being thoughtful about the best way to store and retrieve your items can give you options, now that you've edited out the things you don't use, need or love!

Chapter II: Books

We tend to get very personally attached to our books. Many of us will state that we love our books. We believe that our collection of books, displayed for others to see, says something about us, something that we want to be said about us. Books can be like postcards from our past, as if to say, *"When I read this book, it was an important time; something mattered about it,"* and the book is there to mark its place. Our bookshelves seem to be an homage to our identity, who we have been, who we are now, and whom we thought we might become. No wonder so many barriers come up for us when we are standing before our bookshelves and considering letting go of some:

Future Fear: *"I might want to read this again,"* or *"Someone else might want to read this someday and I'd want to be able to loan this to them if they did."*

Purposeless Practicality: *"This is a good book about [a topic I no longer am interested in]"* or *"These were my textbooks in grad school."*

Sunk Cost: *"I spent a lot of money building on this collection over the years."*

Recoup the Cost: *"This is probably a valuable book. It's a first edition. Aren't those valuable?"*

Guilt: *"This was a gift from a coworker when I left my old job. I haven't read it, but she signed a nice note on the inside."*

Sentimentality: *"I loved this book. Just looking at it makes me smile,"* or *"This was a book of poetry an old flame gave me."*

Perceived value to someone else: *"These were books my children read when they were younger. They might want to read them with their own kids someday or have them for their own memories."*

Whether we are considering reducing our book collection because of space restrictions/needs, or because we are just ready to think differently about the role this collection plays in our current lives, so many barriers can appear! The great irony of books is that their stories can help us escape, but their presence all together can overwhelm and create the need to escape!

Book collections are a category where the debate between *"status quo possession,"* where we only get rid of things when we have a good reason to, and *"purposeful possession,"* where we only KEEP things because we have a good reason to, can get heated. Being able to take a new approach to what we keep and why we keep it can help make progress in reducing a book collection, but it also invites all those barriers into the process!

When we listen for our barriers and understand the *"why"* of our resistance or struggle with this process, we can start to analyze our book collections with more clarity. If you've said to yourself, *"I'm ready to let go of some of this, because it's standing in the way of what I truly want and need for my space,"* it is time to combat the barriers with the questions and facts that can help determine how to reach that goal less painfully.

Again, using the **EEEEZ** method, start with **Excavate**. Books can be a challenging category to excavate, depending on the size of your collection, and the size of your workspace. Perhaps you tackle the whole collection, or just one broad category, or maybe one single title at a time.

Evaluate is the next phase. Some people will have no problem sorting through their books just based on their emotions and their gut feelings. They can just know if there's something about it that feels compelling enough to keep it. For other people, they will work best with logic and practicality to counteract the emotional side.

First, here are some of the practical factors to consider when reviewing books and trying to tear down the barriers:

> 1)   Reference books aren't as relevant as they once were and are increasingly unnecessary with the internet! Old textbooks, *Merriam-Webster Dictionary, Roget's Thesaurus,* and *Bartlett's Familiar Quotations*, or that college paper style-guide book, I'm looking at you. Unless you make your living as a writer, can you think of how or when you might ever use these books again? Even as a writer, don't you just type into an internet search: *synonym for* ____?.
>
> 2)   Reading books more than once is not as likely as it seemed when you finished it in the first place. What percentage of the books you own now have you read more than once? What percentage would you REALLY read more than once, if you

haven't already?

3) Maybe you have an e-reader now, and you download your books. Your collection and preferred reading style is becoming more and more electronic, not on paper. (If you're like me, you love that you can increase the font on the e-reader and actually READ some of those books now!)

4) The reason you bought and read a book may have been very specific to a time or situation in your life that has long since passed. Think of it similarly to a prom dress or a special ingredient you purchased once for a recipe you would never make again. Keeping it around is only about your past, not your present or your future.

5) You may not have actually read some of these books, and some you may never read. There are books on your shelves you had the best intentions of reading. Or finishing. You didn't. Deep down, you know you won't.

6) Instructional or how-to books can serve a purpose, but only if you're in the phase where you still need that instruction, or this is your only source for that information. One example of books in this category is cookbooks. When's the last time you said, *"Hmmm... I'm going to make something new. I should browse through one of these books that I rarely use to see what is in there?"* We use our most-loved books, our treasured written recipe cards, and the internet most of the time. The lesser-loved, lesser-read books came your way and you thought you would use them, but you're not.

7) Books take up a lot of space. If your space is limited, or you are moving to a new space with much less capacity for non-critical items, you may be forced to edit your collection

8) Paperbacks really don't hold up well. The ones you've been saving for a few decades are yellow, dusty, and probably smell a little.

If those practical guidelines seem easy, but you're still stuck, you may instead need to tackle the emotional sides of your barriers head-on:

- Ask yourself: *"Am I keeping this book because it means something to me, or because I think it says something about me to someone (anyone?) else who looks at my shelves? And that feeling is more important to me than the book itself?"* If you have books on your shelf that you know deep down you acquired or kept because you think they make you look smarter, deeper, more well-read, more interesting than you really are, your book collection isn't about your books and is about your identity and self-image.

- Some of your books were a gift from someone else and you're only holding on to them because it was a gift. Maybe you read it and maybe you didn't. But you feel guilty doing anything other than keeping them, because, after all, someone gave it to you, right? Holding onto it purely because it was a gift and you'd feel guilty is not adding anything to your love of books and your love of your book collection.

- For books you've already read, but realistically won't read again, ask yourself why you're keeping them. Is it still important to you to hold onto them, and if so, why? This question is not about how you felt or feel about the book, but rather how keeping it serves your life and your future. Loving the book may not be a reason to keep it any longer.

- For books you started and did not finish or will never make it a priority to read, what is the value they bring to your book collection and your life now? Is it a positive value or a negative one? Do they make you feel good to see them on your shelf, or do they remind you, negatively, of what you haven't accomplished?

- Think about those reference books and the old text books. What do you REALLY need? When you say you really need it, when is the last time you used it? When is the last time you needed that information and you had no other way to get it?

If these guidelines and questions are opening your eyes and helping you tear down your barriers, it is time to plot out your **Edit** strategy on how you will physically get the work done. Maybe you're not going to be ruthless, but you're going to skim a little off the top. Or maybe you attack this in multiple waves. Here are a few tactical strategies to help you take action:

- Divide out your "*yet to read*" pile, review it for whether you're just as interested in it now as you were when you got it, and **give the new pile a realistic expiration date.** Stick to this, and focus on this part of your collection between now and the expiration date. Make these a priority, or let them go.

- **Organize your non-fiction by topic**. You'll see what you have, how many of them you have, and whether that's a realistic collection that is part of what is important to you TODAY, both in topic and in quantity.

- Consider letting go of any reference or instructional non-fiction that **you do not have a real and otherwise irreplaceable role** in your future.

- **Someone else may be at the very place in their lives for your books to be perfect**. Gift them. Donate them. You may even make some money selling some of your books.

- And, okay, I'll just say it: Get rid of the paperbacks that aren't your (small list of) absolute favorites. You'll be able to find organizations out there that will value you them for lending and borrowing, instead of keeping them with you, never to be read again.

Rethinking a book collection, what we keep in it, and why we keep it, is tough. This category has been tough for me and people like me, who grew up with a love for reading, in a house where everyone loved reading. That's why I included them in the five categories to cover in Part II. Letting them go, however, doesn't have to feel like it is only a negative process, like you're mourning each title as it leaves your collection.

I remember speaking with someone one day about how finally he came to let go of his very large and loved book collection: *"I realized I wasn't reading them, and was never going to read them again. Yet they were locked up in here like a prison, when they deserved to be scattered in the world, to be discovered and read by new people. It was time to let them all go."* They weren't serving him anymore, and more importantly, he knew they could serve others. He broke free.

Chapter III: Collections and Memorabilia

This is a companion chapter to Part I, Chapter VI, the sentimentality chapter. It is a guide to help you harvest only the treasures that mean the most to you, to move forward honoring those items, and to release the rest.

Sentimentality is a big barrier here, but it isn't the only barrier we've discussed that can come up in this category. There is also:

Sunk Cost: *"I've invested in a collection over time, and am feeling the tug of that price tag on my heart."*

Recoup the Cost: *"I don't really love these as much as I did when I was actively collecting, and I'd be willing to let go of some of it, as long as I could get what I think they're worth for them. "*

Guilt: *"I feel like letting go of items from my past, especially those tied to memories of others, can feel like a betrayal of them."*

Future Fear: *"I am too afraid I'll lose this memory, even if isn't an important one."*

Beginning a process like this with being clear about what your goals are and what you hope to accomplish can be a great foundation for you to keep your energy and focus strong throughout. You already know this is going to be a shaky process, and you may be doing it more out of necessity than desire, which may mean your brain (driving necessity) and your heart (driving desire) may be at odds with each other.

You've geared yourself up, and you're ready to dive in. So, how do you get started?

Get the right kind of help from the start, if you anticipate you'll need it. This is hard work and can be easy to abandon if you don't have the right kind of partner or help to keep you focused and productive along the way. Do you have someone you can trust on this exercise? Hiring a professional organizer for these psychologically and emotional heavier categories can be an excellent investment in your desire to reach your goals. (Check out www.NAPO.net to identify professional organizers or productivity consultants near you.) You may also have a friend who can be your "decluttering buddy." Either way, you'll want someone who would be willing to go through the items with you, keep you focused and on track to meet your goals, and not judge you for your decisions.

Start small. It's not about tackling everything. It's about addressing some items and making some tough decisions. One box. One drawer. One tin. One bulletin board. Wherever you keep the stuff that you know I'm talking about. Don't let yourself get overwhelmed. Start with one group, finish it, then move to the next.

Starting small can help with managing the overwhelm, but so can limiting your physical interaction with the items. Sometimes, when I work with a client who has a very strong emotional connection to these items, I physically handle the items and place just a few in front of them. They then select what to keep and what to part without touching them. Why? Touching an item can reinforce an emotional connection to it, and makes it harder to imagine releasing it. You know that feeling, where you've completely forgotten a thing existed, for decades, and now that you're reunited with it, it seems massively important? That is the feeling we're trying to anticipate and prevent. With help, you can achieve this separation to help with your decision making, too.

Set space limits. If you've decided that you're editing down your collection because the value of your storage and your real estate is more important to you, then know what that boundary is that you're setting for yourself. One large bin in the basement? One drawer in your nightstand? One box under the bed? Whatever it is, have a good sense of the capacity as you start, so that you can help achieve your vision.

I'm not advocating that the space should always guide how much you can keep, but in this exercise, if you feel you would benefit from the criteria of boundaries, you should experiment with that as a tool.

Give yourself time, but *not TOO much* time. The goal is to edit down what you have. You'll relive some moments while you go, but stay on task, and keep working through the collection.

If you're doing this work on your own, you might consider using a timer, or if you think you can notice the changes in the background, some music ("*I'm going to work on this box for only two songs.*") Your timer can help you with a "*per item*" limit, where you might say that you're only going to touch and revisit an item for a period of 30 seconds or less. You may also use it for larger sets like, *"I'm going to look through this pile of newspaper clippings only for five minutes."* Finally, time limits can help you set boundaries on how much time per sitting you're exposing yourself to for this process. If you decide you need to put work into this project, but are afraid of the overwhelm that can come from it, you can set an alarm for thirty minutes, sixty minutes, whatever you think you can handle. You can then walk away from the session after that and come back another time.

Keeping track of time and setting limits for editing, sorting, etc. can help you stay focused and avoid the rabbit hole of wandering through your past and your memories.

Think seriously about why keeping something is important. This means challenging yourself to not just accept, *"This makes me happy when I look at it,"* especially if you are gathering a pile of 30, 40, 50 items that all make you happy. Yes, it is memorable, and makes you feel good, but is it IMPORTANT? And, again, sometimes it brings about negative feelings, and you should always question why you're holding onto things that make you feel sad, angry, hurt, or any other negative emotions that can come with difficult memories and the memorabilia tied to them.

Using possessions as tools to recapture or generate emotions is one of the ways in which we justify that sentimental items are *"useful."* But in that view, we can have items that are redundant. I worked with a client who was struggling with his collection of papers he'd written in college, more than twenty years ago. He didn't have a career in the field he studied back then, and admitted that, even if he were in that field, he wouldn't be referring to these as resources. But when he looked at them now, he was proud of them; they reflected hard work and his growth in his thinking and his expression of thought over time. There were two dozen of these papers. I challenged him to consider whether keeping only ONE paper that he was most proud of would change the emotional reaction that looking at (but never reading) all twenty-five did. He understood that seeing twenty-five didn't make him more proud than having just one did. He could generate the same pride, if he wanted to, with just his most prized paper, with the best grade and feedback from the professor, and the only one he actually recalled writing.

Another client and I were going through greeting cards from her daughter's christening, ten years earlier. Her original thought had been *"Everyone who sent us a gift or card will always be important to us. My daughter will want to appreciate who honored her."* As she looked through the cards, it was full of ones from people she hadn't spoken to in years, some she couldn't even remember. She announced, *"If these aren't important to me today, why would I ever think they'd be important to her?"* She kept about 10% of them, ones that not only were from treasured friends and family, but the ones who had handwritten notes to her in them. *"I don't need to have a copy of their autograph and nothing else with it."*

Consider breaking up a collection. A collection tends to feel larger than the sum of its parts. You can collect items that have something in common, like special figurines or beer steins, or items that are a physical representation of a hobby you enjoy (*"I love building model airplanes"* or *"These are all the medals from every race I've been in"*). It can be a struggle to imagine letting go of parts of it, but it can also be liberating, and a wonderful way to revisit what you loved about your collection in the first place.

Choosing to harvest only your favorites can be a way to actually improve the quality of your collection by not focusing on the quantity. I worked with a client who had loved horses and had a collection of horse figurines on a shelf. There were many of them, and she looked and was able to say, *"I don't love them all. I don't need to keep ones I don't love, just because they happen to be with the others."* She was able to find criteria as she went through them: ones that were broken could go, ones that she didn't like the looks of their painted or carved faces could go, etc. She cut her collection in half very quickly, and beamed with pride as she looked at the ones that remained, the ones she truly cared about.

An exercise that can help with this is one popularized in *Conquering Chronic Disorganization*, by Judith Kohlberg. In this, she discusses the sorting and evaluating technique, *"Friends, Acquaintances, Strangers."* This approach is very useful for sorting through large collections of items to narrow down to your favorites. Friends are the most loved, the most used, your go-to items. Friends stay. Strangers are the ones you care about and use the least; they may even be ones you resent! Strangers have no business staying. Acquaintances are in the middle. While some percentage may stay, it might be more out of necessity than desire. Ultimately, many acquaintances, *"these are still good*" items, may find their way out the door.

Think about the things you've collected, even if they seem like they're a set and you wouldn't otherwise dream of breaking the set up. Focus on what rule you think there is in place that is preventing you from doing that? Yes, you really can just hold onto one teacup from a set. The world won't end, and you'll love looking at one teacup on your shelf so much more than knowing that 12 teacups that you used to enjoy are in a box in the basement somewhere.

Do what you need to do to remember that these are things, not memories, not people. Your heart will swell and you'll be reminiscing as you go through items. There may even be times where you're not reacting emotionally, but merely acknowledging moments on the timeline of your life (*"Oh, these were the brochures for the places we thought we'd visit on the way to see the Grand Canyon."*)

Just as we talked about the difference between things being memorable and important, also keep in mind that **the items are things, and not the memories themselves**. Would you have forgotten that you went to the Grand Canyon if you didn't have the brochure?

You may need a mantra, *"This is not a memory. The memory is in my head and my heart, not in a thing."*

The same goes for items that you come across that you've inherited from others. If you've inherited other people's passions and priorities, you may be struggling with separating the thing from your feelings about the person. Do you have other items that remind you of this person? Could you keep a few items you truly appreciate, but not all of them? Can you continue to make space in your heart for this person without making space in your home for his or her belongings?

Honor what you're keeping. Is this process reintroducing you to things that mean a ton to you, bring you joy, make you smile when you see them? Now, how do you feel about putting them back in a box, not remembering them again until the next time you do this work? Consider ways in which you can capture that positive feeling that seeing one of these items brings you on a more permanent basis. Small arrangements can be displayed in shadow boxes or on a shelf. Photos of items can be placed where you will see them regularly and they will make you smile. There are many ways to do this, but honoring an item is essentially the opposite of *"stays forgotten for decades in a box in the attic."*

Write down the stories of why the items are important. If you really want to keep it, mainly because you want someone else to inherit it, take some time to capture your thoughts for posterity. A trinket someone else inherits without context can easily be viewed as expendable. Help your family appreciate your legacy and value what you hold dear.

Create a "time capsule" for items you're not quite ready to let go of *just* yet, but you're warming up to the idea. Put aside a collection in a bin or a box, and vow to give it real thought about letting go. Put an appointment on your calendar for a period of time, such as six months, into the future to remind yourself of this commitment. If you haven't had a reason to think about the items or go looking for them for six months, you may feel more comfortable letting go at that time.

Finally, clean the items and the location in which they live. Sometimes, these can be a bit dusty. If they're important to you, take care of them so that you can preserve them well and longer.

Sentimental items can take many rounds of work. You might go through everything now and then not come back for months. Future rounds of review will help you gain clarity on what is not just memorable but is important and has a role in your current life and your future.

As you continue to rediscover and display items that are important, you'll feel the difference between the important and the trivial growing. You continue to harvest only the best, only the most important items that reflect the memories of your life, and get to a point where you can sit with them, reflect on them, and share them in the easiest ways possible. You let go of saying *"I have lots of things I love. They're in the attic and the basement and I haven't seen them in years. But knowing they are in the house is good enough."* You crave having the best out, and you can let go of the bulk of the unimportant items around them which require the entire lot to be stored out of sight. Start small, with the best-intended goals, and make progress, one item at a time.

Chapter IV: Photographs

There's typically just one BIG barrier when it comes to photos: **Sentimentality**. *"I remember this..."* Of course, other barriers can arise:

Purposeless Practicality: *"Even though I have 20 different shots of this same sunset, they're all such nice pictures."*

Guilt: *"I'm kind of the person in my family who people think of as responsible for the photos and the stories of our history. People have handed them down to me and trusted me with them. I'd feel guilty if I let go of photos and someone else wants them or would have enjoyed them later."*

Photos are wonderful, right? So why would you tackle reducing your photos? What problems may you be facing?

- You can't find what you want, when you want it (paper photos or digital photos).

- You have photos in multiple places and have difficulty keeping track of them all.

- You're downsizing or moving to a space where you just have too much of this category, and it would be better if it took up less space.

- You're divorcing and need to address ownership of the photos in the future.

- You're concerned about losing your photos to physical damage, loss, or file corruption and want to make sure the most important photos are preserved.

- You want your family and generations in the future to know the stories behind the pictures, or at the very least, the names of the people that might be considered important, that they wouldn't otherwise recognize.

If you are facing a compelling reason to make your collection one that solves your problem and brings you great happiness and pride, then it is time to tackle the photo collection.

There are two kinds of challenging photo collections out there today:

> 1) Mostly printed photos, whether in scrapbooks or albums or piles of loose photos in boxes, drawers, trunks, etc. There may be some digital, but that's not the real challenge you face.

> 2) Mostly digital photos, in sources such as your computer, backed up on disks and drives, in the cloud, on social media, or stuck on your phone. There may be some printed photos, which may or may not be an issue like the first, but certainly not near the size and future growth trajectory of your digital photos.

Of course, you could also be struggling equally with both.

Knowing your challenge can help you focus your effort and energy on the collections that need your attention the most. The approaches here work for either type of photo, but it can be a little trickier to work with digital, purely because you're not physically creating piles as you evaluate. You may wish to set up folders as you work through your decision-making process. Don't be afraid of the delete button when you come across something you know can be eliminated immediately.

Reviewing your photos involves being critical about what you keep and how you keep them. Decluttering photos (in print or digital) takes some good rules up front, if you believe you can't rely on your gut feelings to help you achieve your goals. There are no right or wrong answers, but they help to draw a line in the sand about what to keep and what to part with.

Our photos tell stories we want to remember. Maybe they even are just artwork, beautiful to look at. But not all of them serve us in this way. Some are just images that we don't love, need, or value in any way. Some are just things we have acquired and kept, for no compelling reason at all. The process of editing our photos allows us to separate the valuable from the space-taking, so that we can best harvest our most important images.

The method I recommend for reviewing and prioritizing is the "**A / B / C drawer**" sorting system. Imagine a filing cabinet with three drawers, where the top is A, middle is B, and bottom is C. Drawer A is the most convenient and should hold our most important items, C is least convenient and should hold our least important items (the ones we've decided to keep at all). There will be plenty that we're not keeping; think of that as a D Drawer – for discard, dispose, delete!

As you begin sorting through photos, whether digital or printed, start to evaluate what would be in each category, based on their importance to you.

- **A Drawer:** "This is a treasure. I can't imagine living without this. If it were destroyed in a disaster, I would be devastated."
- **B Drawer:** "I enjoy this picture, it means something to me, and I believe it would mean something to others if they came across it. The memories it conjures up are meaningful ones, and it fills my heart when I see it. They tell my important stories."
- **C Drawer:** "It's a good enough picture, but I wouldn't miss it if it weren't around anymore. This may include photos from events of which I have plenty of other shots that are better to keep." Ultimately, this group should be pretty thin. After all, if it isn't important or meaningful, it may not warrant the space it takes.

What doesn't make it to a drawer at all, or goes to the D Drawer? Photos that are blurry, are thumbs, are ones of yourself that you absolutely hate and have no other redeeming quality in it, of events that weren't meaningful and you don't cherish, of events or people you simply can't place or remember, and the silly selfies, fun shots, and screenshots that are a dime a thousand from your phone. The discard pile may also include doubles (though, share with someone else who might love it, if it is a very special photo).

This sorting method can help us visually imagine piles and prioritization among our items. We won't store them in a three-drawer filing cabinet; this is just language to help you visualize distance and placement of items relative to each other. For example, the "drawers" may be:

- **A Drawer:** displayed on our bookshelf in the living room. Most important ones are probably scanned and backed up, to preserve them.
- **B Drawer:** located a box on a shelf in our home office,

accessible if it is needed quickly. These may be scanned, especially if we want to create digital photo books out of them, or at the very least, have a copy in case something happens to the original.

- **C Drawer:** stored in a box in the closet in a spare bedroom. These probably don't need to be backed up, because they're the least important of what we have, but it's fine if they are.

The categories may seem straightforward enough and many are going to feel like obvious choices, but what about some of the harder ones, or the ones that are on the edge of two drawers, or the ones that may end up in Discard? Some other questions to ask yourself:

- **Do you have multiple shots?** How many photos from an event do you truly need? If you have 10 photos of your child and a birthday cake, do you need all 10? How many is *"enough"* for you to say you've held onto the images that remind you of a day that was important? (I'm not even suggesting you don't need pictures from *all* the birthdays... that's yours to evaluate!)

- **Is it still as meaningful**? In the moment that you took the photo, it was meaningful. Is it still as meaningful now, and if so, why? If it is still meaningful, how many captures of any individual moment do you need? Keep in mind, we took photos of tourist sights and places before the internet, because we thought it would be the only way to revisit a sight after we've left.

- **Is it art?** Are you drawn to this because you enjoy looking at the image, or because it is capturing something that is important to you? Some photos are just plain art, and that's fine! If you truly love looking at it for its artistic purposes, you should hold onto it. If you have 10 shots of the same thing, all wonderful and lovely, however, could you generate that feeling you get when you see ONE of the pictures?

- **Is it someone else's memories:** Sometimes, the photos

collected are from someone else's experiences. Is this YOUR memories or someone else's? Sometimes photos are portraits, *"This is your grandfather, when he was in the Navy."* Sometimes, the photo is someone else's memory, *"These are photos from when your grandfather was in the South Pacific and was on a side trip."* They're not of him, just photos from the trip he took. These are his memories, not yours. Are you holding onto sets of photos that are not of your own experiences? If, so, why?

Someday, I will inherit the photos my parents have, and I'll use this guideline. There are many from a trip that they went on when they were dating. When I go through them in the future, I will keep the pictures of my parents from that day, but let go of the pictures of their friends, whom I have never met, whom my parents haven't seen in fifty years. My parents enjoy them and should keep them now. But when they become intermingled with my possessions some day in the future, the importance changes.

Your collection of photos is your museum. You must manage and curate your collection if you want to enjoy it effortlessly in the future. If you want others to enjoy it without you guiding them through it, help make that happen now. Far too often family members are handed a trunk full of faded photos, full of mysterious faces and landscapes. They find it overwhelming and heartbreaking, as if they were handed a box of puzzle pieces without a picture to follow. They want nothing more than to put that puzzle together, but they can't. It doesn't have to be that way, and this chapter is the way to make sure it doesn't.

Chapter V: Paperwork

Paperwork, either in paper or digital form, is a necessity in life. There's little getting around that. However, the answers to the "*keep*" questions – what do we keep, why do we keep it, how do we keep it, and for how long do we keep it – are very different today than it was in the 20th century. With the common technology in our lives today, email, electronic banking, scanners, and online accounts, the many ways we can access information today mean all of those "*keep*" questions may deserve new answers.

Paperwork is also one of the biggest complaints that professional organizers hear about when we speak with people about what isn't working in their home, or what drives them crazy. Here are some of the top problems I hear about when complaining about paper:

- You can't find what you need, when you need it.
- You are incurring late fees and penalties from unpaid bills because you didn't keep track of the paper or the task.
- You miss important dates or opportunities because you've lost track of your paper.
- You have run out of space for how much paper you can save.
- Your management of paperwork is creating stress for your relationship or career.

When these problems exist, it can be a call to action that it is time to edit down your piles of paperwork and change your paper processing system. Again, some barriers arrive, just in time to stop you in your tracks:

Future Fear: *"But what if I need this someday?"* is the most common barrier when it comes to paperwork and files. We imagine that someday we might need something and that this is the only source for it.

Sentimentality: *"These are all my old birthday cards/ school papers/report cards/kids' artwork"* and so on. The collection of papers serves only to represent or document our past.

Want to Dispose of Safely or Smartly: *"Does this need to be shredded?"*

Purposeless Practicality: *"This coupon is still good"* or *"I might want to look into this someday."*

All of these are surmountable barriers, and you can tame or even conquer each one as you face them. It may require a closer look at to your specific *"why"* when it comes to holding onto different categories of paper. Here are a few examples:

Some people keep paper because they don't trust institutions. They believe that if they let go of a piece of paper and a company comes back to them and says they owe money or didn't do something they were supposed to do, they can't prove it isn't true. The truth is very rarely do those *"what if?"* events come up, and certainly not in proportion to the amount of paper people still hold. The problem situation exists when someone's instinct tends to be, "*I'd rather hold onto 1000 pieces of paper, if it justifies that I had the one that I needed in the pile,*" and paper takes over the house.

Some people keep paper because they fear being audited, when someone proclaims that you must provide evidence that you didn't do anything wrong. They will keep everything, even if it's not tax-related, out of fear that EVERY piece of paper that has to do with money that was spent is critical. Again, if someone is saving items from an overabundance of fear, and papers that aren't even helpful for an audit, it can be a problem. Sitting with a tax accountant to review the situation can help dissect irrational fear from a smart and safe plan.

Sometimes, people keep paper because it helps them be a resource of information, either because they want to be helpful, or maybe because they want to be proven right and think of paper as evidence. They keep things to get their hands on it "*just in case*" they want to refer to it again if a topic comes up. Their personal library is there to tap into if they ever need it again. These kinds of papers include recipe files, home improvement ideas, workout plans, medical advice, magazine articles, appliance manuals, etc.

Many keep paper because it genuinely comforts them to see the life they have lived. It is more of a museum than a functional system. It may even be hyper-organized, and they can tell you everything about it. It is a badge of honor for them.

Finally, some people keep paper because they believe every scrap of paper is equally important to the next, and all are of critical importance. (*Note: this person may be suffering from hoarding disorder. This chapter, this book, is not intended to address someone in this situation.*)

All of these examples illustrate some of the many ways in which we are motivated to hold onto paper. For those who identify with these challenges, and also find their problems outlined on the chapter's first page, it may be time to address the paperwork and reset the needs, wants, and the systems that support it.

We'll discuss three key areas of managing paper:

1) Reviewing the paper you have throughout your home and whether you will keep it all.

2) Processing incoming paper to identify and complete actions

3) Setting up a filing system that works for short- and long-term storage

First, you'll start with reviewing the paper that exists in your home already. Whether your system needs a complete overhaul or you're looking to make updates based on how your needs have changed, this project needs a plan, some guidelines, and bins for shredding and recycling. It may also feel like it gets worse before it gets better, so patience is key!

This is another project in which the **EEEEZ** method can be very helpful.

- **Excavate:** Gather your paper piles and files to ensure you've found everything. You may do this in one category at a time.
- **Evaluate:** Determine the guidelines you'll use for what is necessary to keep, and what isn't
- **Edit:** Follow the rules set up in Evaluate, and act on your plan, making progress to completion
- **Establish Zones**: Create the right system for yourself to help receive, process, and either dispose of or store paper for future retrieval.

Excavate: This may mean gathering piles from around your home all at once, or a bit at a time. You'll want to make sure you've got room to work, on tables, the floor, the couch, wherever! You also may want to have post-it notes so you can start to label some piles as you sort. You may end up doing this in a few waves; for those of you who aspire to be a *"touch something once"* kind of person, you may not have that luxury here.

Evaluate: This process has two steps. The first is just deciding if a piece of paper falls in the category of KEEP or TOSS. The second is refining the *"flavor"* within each of those to identify the next action or final home of the item.

When deciding whether something goes in a KEEP pile or a TOSS pile, some decisions will be obvious to you (sale circulars from last month? Toss. Birth Certificate? Keep) but others may require more research. Check with your tax accountant for guidance, or search the internet for *"how long to keep documentation."* There are a lot of great resources out there that can help you with this, so I won't go through them here. Remember that internet lists are likely to be conservative, encouraging you to keep more than you need, and with technology changing, advice may even be antiquated.

Generally, however, I want you to keep in mind a few criteria when you're going to determine if they are KEEP or TOSS:

> 1) Necessity: What is the situation that will come up that will require you to present this information again? Think about this when you come across papers from old jobs, college, etc.
>
> 2) Access: Can you get this again elsewhere if you didn't have the paper, even if it took a little effort?
>
> 3) Importance: Does the item hold true importance for personal reasons or because it generates future action, or is it just memorable?

Think also about what has changed in your lifetime with regards to paper records. So much of what is important today is available electronically or you can scan and save digitally. This wasn't the case when many of us began learning the guidelines about what to keep and how long to keep them. It may require some extra steps if it's not readily available, such as contacting the institution for assistance with back invoices, but the likelihood of needing these statements gets smaller each day.

Pay stubs are another great example of how times have changed. We used to get pay stubs attached to actual paychecks, and hold onto them until the end of the year and validate that the amount reported on our W2 was accurate. Today, with direct deposit and the systems available for both processing payroll and for retrieving your statement, your need to hold onto a piece of paper each pay period has diminished if not evaporated.

The second part of **Evaluate** is a review that goes a bit deeper, down to the next level within TOSS and KEEP. Here are the next level down *"flavors"* and their guidelines:

> 1) TOSS/RECYCLE: anything you're discarding that does not have personal identification information on it, and the material is recyclable.
>
> 2) TOSS/SHRED: any paperwork you are discarding that has personally identifiable information on it, not just name and address, but something that can be tied to your identification or private information.
>
> 3) TOSS/TRASH: anything you're discarding that does not have personal identification information, and the material is *not* recyclable.
>
> 4) KEEP/ACT: any piece of paper that triggers an *"I need to do something with this"* thought, such as pay, RSVP, fill out a form, send to someone, make a call, etc., it goes in this pile to be dealt with after sorting. When you're done with the action, you'll consider which pile KEEP or TOSS pile it goes in.
>
> 5) KEEP/IMPORTANT INFORMATION: a pile will be revisited when you begin working with your filing structure and you have the room to create more narrowly sorted piles.
>
> 6) KEEP/SENTIMENTAL OR PERSONAL: papers that are important to you for sentimental reasons, but do not have future life ramifications, e.g. certificates of achievement, letters and greeting cards, magazine articles, school papers. For the sentimental, you'll use the same method from the Memorabilia/ Collections Chapter to

sort through these, and wade through the practical and emotional criteria to determine their future.

Edit: Putting those rules to work that you outlined in **Evaluate** is the next step. Since much of the tedious work and critical thinking is done in this phase, this is the one that requires the most patience and time. Pace yourself and recognize that going through paper can take longer than you might imagine.

Start going through your papers and laying out your piles. By all means, your shred and recycling piles can go straight into receptacles meant for that. You probably won't spend time shredding as you're editing, but it's a good idea to think about what you WILL do with shredding. Are you shredding at home? Do you have a time set aside for when that will happen? Do you need to find a company or store that will shred for you? Make that time in your calendar. Living with piles indefinitely is not getting you closer to living without chaos.

Establish Zones: Clearing out your piles and files and drawers can be a cathartic and rewarding process. You gain back space, maybe from multiple places, and sometimes you uncover important paperwork you thought was lost. But that's only part of the way to organization. The rest is in making sure you establish the systems and processes for the other two important aspects of paper management: Processing paper-based actions, and filing paper away for short-term or long-term in a way that supports retrieval. We'll go through each of those to explore how to establish those zones.

Processing paper-based actions. Dealing with papers as they come in your home, and triaging between what requires action and what doesn't, is the first part of managing paperwork in your home. If you have the luxury of a lot of space for filing paper in the place where you actually process home administration work, that's great, but not everyone does.

A paper processing system needs to rely on routines and habits which allow for the identification of the important actions, and the elimination of the unimportant paperwork. Some steps to incorporate:

    1) Check your paper sources (typically mail and kids' backpacks) every day, and eliminate the items that don't even need to make it into a pile in the first place. Have a shred and a recycle station

convenient, and immediately remove the items that don't require action and aren't KEEP-worthy, before they even hit the kitchen counter.

2) Deal with the paper that comes into your home with regular frequency. While you probably don't need to deal with every piece of paper every day, you want to address it at least weekly so it doesn't pile up and become overwhelming.

Set up a space or container which helps you sort the incoming paper. Consider an inbox system in a convenient place, with the most common action-driven categories. The categories that often work for people: PAY, ACT, FILE.

Pay: *"I have to pay this, and when I'm ready to pay bills, I'll grab these."*

Act: *"I need to do something with this — fill out a form, make a call, send an email, research something; I'll need to set time aside to move this forward."*

File: *"I need to keep this, either short-term or longer-term, but no other action is necessary right now."*

Some people may have other categories; the **For Someone Else** category for items you're setting aside for someone else's attention. The **Read Later** category is for papers that don't require an important action, but they're not going to be kept long-term. It's something you want to pay attention to, may discard when you're done with it, but you want to set it aside to review.

3) Set up a routine that helps you move each of those categories in your inbox system forward. Purposeful piles are great, but if they just grow, things will get neglected and lost. Determine a frequency that will help you move through these categories successfully. Will you PAY bills every week? Do you review ACT twice a week? Do you take the FILE pile once a month to deal with? Put a recurring appointment in your calendar to help you stay on top of this routine.

4) Reduce the amount of paper you receive in the first place. Consider going to a paperless or less-paper system, unless there's

an absolute reason you <u>need</u> to have paper for your investment accounts, bank statements, credit cards, mortgage, loans, insurance, utility bills, etc.

If you are a VERY tactile or visual person, this may not work for you. A tactile or visual person might say, *"I will never actually pay my bill unless the mail carrier brings me a piece of paper telling me to do so,"* or *"I don't trust the company or the system and holding onto this paper gives me security that can't be created in any other way."* You may consider however setting up some auto-pay options to help relieve you of the pressure of having to remember.

Where all this collecting, sorting, and acting work happens may need a spot. You may have a few options:

- At your home's hub spot/command center. It's where you'll likely pay bills, fill out forms, and mail them. It's where you act and then discard, or act and then file.

- In the home office. They may be in here for short-term storage, for processing the actions, and then move into your filing system.

- A more portable solution. You don't have a specific home where things live and get done, but you have a tote or basket that you bring with you when you move from one spot of the house to another. Your inbox of paper to be reviewed and your ACT files live in there.

With dedicated space, regular routines, and reliable habits, your ability to stay on top of the incoming paper and complete your actions will help reduce the overwhelm of your daily and weekly paperwork clutter problem.

Finally, we address how to set up your filing system. To establish priorities and zones related to your filing system, we'll use the **A/B/C Drawer** approach again to determine location. (This exercise may translate directly to actual filing cabinet drawers.) The items you've kept in your KEEP/IMPORTANT INFORMATION pile from the Edit phase will end up here. Your KEEP/ACT pile may also be here, as, space-wise, it may be an overlap with your processing paper-based actions.

- **A Drawer:** These are your hottest files, your current working files, and your ACT paperwork. These are items that you need to get your hands on in the *current* time period. They might live in a specific spot on a surface or desktop or even vertical space, or they could physically be in a drawer. The location will be based on your options and your preferences. Do you need to see everything because *"out of sight, out of mind?"* Or do you need to have a neat and streamlined look, and closed storage appeals to you? Once you take action on the papers in this space, they'll move to either a different drawer, or be discarded.

- **B Drawer:** This is your mid-term storage. Mid-term storage is for items that are current in your life, and you may need to access on a regular occasion, either to take out of the file or put into the file. They don't need to be at your fingertips and always exposed, however. These might include this year's receipts for taxes, files for active accounts like current loans, paperwork related to your children's current school year, or your current insurance policy. After the year ends, you can look through each folder to see if you need to keep items within there, and remove the papers that are no longer is important.

- **C Drawer:** Longer term storage. Things you don't need to access unless an unusual situation comes up, but you have determined are important to keep and be retrievable. These would include old tax returns, discharged loan paperwork, real estate transaction information, old disability files, divorce paperwork, health records, etc. These are things you need to keep, but don't need to have in your *active* space. These may be stored in watertight totes in a basement, a filing cabinet in a closet, etc. For really important documents, you may even use a safety deposit box at the bank.

Not all your files NEED to be in the same room. They *may* be better organized for the way you want to live when they're located separately.

Setting up the bones of a successful filing system means creating one that makes it easy to put papers away where they are supposed to go and easy to find what you need when you're looking for it.

- It's easy to get into and out of, to put items in or take items out, not jam-packed or in a tricky location.

- It's labeled in a meaningfully way, making sense to you when you read them, and are in a logical order that aligns with how your brain works. The words need to make sense to YOU. While I might use "*House*" someone else might use a "*Home Sweet Home*" label. Just make it meaningful for *you*.

- It's located in a place you don't hate spending time in. If you hate being in the space, you're not likely to want to keep up on your filing there.

- It works with your visual and tactile preferences to help make the aspects of filing and retrieving easier, including the furniture or container that holds your files, the folders or organizers you use, the colors you use, the order you establish, and how visible things need to be.

That "KEEP/IMPORTANT INFORMATION" pile from the Edit process goes through refinement here as you Establish Zones for each type of information. You'll take that pile and then sort into more meaningful categories that will help you create your filing system. These could be major headings like House, Banking, Credit Cards, Investments, Auto, Health and Medical, Personal Documents, Educational documents, etc.

There is no right answer, but find the right groups that are relevant to your life. You'll want to take steps to avoid categories that are too broad or too narrow. Too broad means you can't find things inside it. Too narrow means you really need to know the exact label you used when you set it up if you have a chance of finding it again.

Too Broad: "*STUFF RELATED TO OUR HOUSE*"

Too Narrow: House > Basement > Appliances > Furnace > Four Separate Folders for: Warranty, Annual Inspection, Manual, Filter Receipts

It may not always be obvious that one folder, and not four separate ones, will suffice. *"Furnace"* inside *"House"* can be just fine to hold items, especially ones you may never retrieve again.

As you move through your categories, from the broad to the more specific, create groups that go together, and consider the order you'd place them in your filing system. Should *"house"* be first? Or is *"financial"* a category you tend to access for filing or retrieval more often? It doesn't have to be alphabetical. Again, *there is no right answer*; it just needs to make sense to you and your preferences.

Once you have set up this order, you can create folders and labels, and start filing away! You'll also want to put yearly reminders in your calendar for an annual review of those folders, what is in them and do you still keep it? This maintenance helps keep your filing system working for you, not against you!

Paperwork can be overwhelming, whether dealing with the paper that's already around you, or the fact that it seems to just... keep... coming! I hear all the time from clients who are overwhelmed and can't see a way to get unburied from the paper around them; they've reached a point where they've given up. This chapter provides tools to bring hope back to your world!

Conclusion

Breaking free from our stuff is hard, and none of us are immune to the barriers that keep us from doing so, even when we know we should.

Not too long ago, I said goodbye to a rocking chair, the one I had as a toddler. It was a gift from my godfather, who always gave me wonderful gifts, and who passed away at a very young age when I was 15. It was well taken care of, and the cushions had been recovered somewhere along the line. Even though I didn't have a use for it, I had held on to it for years. For as long as I'd had the chair as an adult, it had been stored away. A storage closet in the basement in my last home, on the top shelf in my garage in my current home. It was wrapped in plastic and protected.

When my parents downsized and they gave me the chair, I was 33 and hadn't met my husband yet. My future family life was still yet to be written. *"Well, I might have a daughter. I'll keep it for her."* Then, I met my husband, and our life doesn't include children. Now, the future sitter in that chair wouldn't be my child, and I knew my sister would not have children, either. New vision: *"Well, my best friend might have a daughter, and I'd give it to her."* She's got two awesome boys, and rocking chairs would not be their thing. Then, *"Well, maybe my sister-in-law will have a daughter."* Instead, I've got an adorable nephew. The years went by, and the excuses for me to hold onto this, and turn it into something that someone I love might also love, quickly faded.

Yet the chair remained, in the top corner of my garage, where it sat for five years until this one day, when I was ready to let it go.

The previous year, I almost let it go. My husband talked me out of it. *"You don't seem ready. You're saying you're ready, but you don't seem ready. It's not in the way or anything. It can stay."* He wasn't wrong. So, it stayed.

This time, however, when we started to clean up the garage, it was the very first thing I said. *"Take down the rocking chair for me, and put it at the curb, please."* No discussion. I was ready. It was time. *"Are you sure?"* he asked. *"Yes. I'm sure. If no one takes it from the curb, then I'll figure out what I'll do with it, but it's time."*

A few minutes later, a minivan started to apply the brakes; the driver had caught sight of the chair. She pulled over and came over to look at it.

"Are you giving this away?" she asked, seeming both incredulous and hopeful.

"I am giving it away, yes. It's yours if you'd like it. It was mine when I was little. Now it should be someone else's."

"Thank you so much!" She was obviously thrilled.

And off it went in the back of a minivan.

I took a deep breath and held it. I shed a few tears. However, I was relieved. My internal debate of keep vs. not keep was officially over and out of my hands. Someone was going to have a great day, because she was going to get a great rocking chair in her room. A mom could bring something her child will love into her room, for free. And I got to let go of a thing which wasn't adding any value to my life; it was only a source of… A source of what?

That was the part that was hard. Why was this so tough for me to get rid of? What were the emotions I was battling? What were MY barriers? Because it wasn't REALLY about a rocking chair, so what was it? I explored my own resistance:

- **Guilt:** We have no regrets in our lives for not having children, but I do have guilt over not giving my parents a grandchild. And this chair embodied the guilt I feel towards my parents for not giving them a grandchild, which they really wish they had.

- **Sentimentality and more guilt:** It was something that reminded me of my godfather, who was kind and generous, and died way too young. And part of me felt that holding onto it helped to honor him and the unjustness of his early death. But I also have some smaller things that I have not only held onto, but I proudly display in my home, and I see them every day. Important items and memories of people should be honored and displayed, not wrapped in a plastic bag in the back of the top shelf of the garage for years and years.

- **Perceived value to someone else:** From *"I'll give this to my child"* to *"someone else will love this,"* I felt like it was important to me that the person who would receive it would be important to me, too. If that happened, he or she could value it in the same way I did, understanding why it was special to me. But there was never really that person who magically filled that spot in my life, and someone who didn't know me certainly COULD love it just as much, even if my history wasn't a part of why. I just couldn't imagine dropping it off at a donation center, like I did a million other things. I needed to see the face of any new owner.

So, it took me a long time, and ultimately, years of decluttering other items, before I could tackle the biggest item around. I'm not someone who holds onto large items for sentimental reasons, especially if not displayed or used in some manner. That one thing kept staring back at me, and worse, I had no real reason to get rid of it. It wasn't in the way of anything. It wasn't broken. It wasn't causing me a problem. Those are the status quo possession answers: *"I don't have a good reason to get rid of it, so it must be fine not to."* The fact that it wasn't causing me a problem meant I didn't have to face my feelings about it.

But I've shifted over time to much more purposeful possession. Simply put, if something is not adding to my life, it's taking away from it, whether that's in space or negative emotions. This wasn't a positive part of my life anymore. It became something I knew I needed to deal with, and kept putting off dealing with it, and the eventual action I would need to take loomed over me every time I saw it. What could be less *"adding value"* than that?

It may be uncomfortable or painful or sad to get to the bottom of why you're holding onto things, but you know when it must be done, just as I did. Whether your goals are very specific, like you're downsizing and moving to a smaller home and need to minimize your belongings by half, or they're lifestyle changes, like trying to live a less stressful, less chaotic life, you know it's the right thing to do. That's why it's hard. It's okay to let go of the thing, acknowledge the emotions, and move on to your next chapter, with the things you love and use now. Because, it's never about the stuff, and when you understand that, you'll finally break free from it.

APPENDIX: Clever Girl's Cheat Sheet

8 Questions you can ask yourself to help you untangle the *"I Might Need It Someday"* barrier and break free:

1) When is the last time I used this?

2) How often do I use it and why? Will this still be the case in the future? (e.g. if you use items for hosting Thanksgiving, will you still be hosting in the future?)

3) Do I own another item that can serve the same purpose? Or is it easy for me to borrow from someone else?

4) Is it in good shape, or does it need to be repaired or replaced soon? Is it worth spending the money to repair?

5) Do I know someone else (or could someone else be identified) that could get more use and value out of it now than I am?

6) Is it something I truly love, and has sentimental value that cannot be replaced?

7) Do I own it because it represents another version of me, from the past or an imaginary future, and not who I am today?

8) What is the worst thing that can happen if I let go of this?

Printed in Great Britain
by Amazon